Entertainment Media in Indonesia

Entertainment media now comprise one of the world's largest industries, yet they remain one of the least studied aspects of contemporary mass media. Every day hundreds of millions of people watch television programmes that might broadly be described as 'entertainment', notably in the rapidly developing countries of Asia. However we still have little idea of what drives the production of Asian entertainment television, how audiences engage with television or how political and social élites understand the impact of television on the massive audiences. While India and China have attracted recent media attention, Indonesia has remained largely unnoticed. As Indonesia has the largest Muslim population in the world, is engaged in rapid modernization and the transition to democracy in significant part through the mass media, serious attention is long overdue.

The topics covered include:

- talent shows,
- crime and supernatural Reality TV,
- travel programmes,
- talent quests, and
- popular music.

This book, with contributions from recognized experts on Indonesian media, is therefore of particular importance not just for explaining what is going on in Indonesian popular television, but also for establishing a theoretical framework for the study of entertainment media in other societies. The collection is essential for anyone wishing to know about entertainment media, Asian television and contemporary approaches to the study of Asian mass and popular media.

This book was previously published as a special issue of the *Asian Journal of Communication*.

Mark Hobart is the founder of the Centre for Media and Film Studies, SOAS.

Richard Fox is Assistant Professor of the History of Religions at the University of Chicago Divinity School.

Entertainment Media in Indonesia

Edited by
Mark Hobart and Richard Fox

Routledge
Taylor & Francis Group

LONDON AND NEW YORK

First published 2008 by Routledge

2 Park Square, Milton Park, Abingdon, Oxon OX14 4RN
711 Third Avenue, New York, NY 10017, USA

Routledge is an imprint of the Taylor & Francis Group, an informa business

First issued in paperback 2016

Typeset in Minion by Datapage International Ltd., Dublin, Ireland

British Library Cataloguing in Publication Data
A catalogue record for this book is available from the British Library

ISBN 13: 978-0-415-45117-8 (hbk)
ISBN 13: 978-1-138-96885-1 (pbk)

Contents

Introduction: Why is Entertainment Television in Indonesia Important?
Mark Hobart   vii

1. The Foreignizing Gaze: Producers, Audiences, and
   Symbols of the 'Traditional'
   Gareth Barkin   1

2. Fame, Fortune, *Fantasi*: *Indonesian Idol* and the New Celebrity
   Penelope Coutas   20

3. Entertaining Illusions: How Indonesian Élites Imagine Reality
   TV Affects the Masses
   Mark Hobart   42

4. Dangdut Soul: Who are 'the People' in Indonesian Popular Music?
   Andrew N. Weintraub   60

5. Afterword
   Richard Fox   81

Index   89

Introduction: Why is Entertainment Television in Indonesia Important?

Mark Hobart

This special edition about contemporary entertainment media in Indonesia consists of four articles. Each focuses on different popular genres of entertainment on television and their associated commentaries, primarily in the print media. The authors examine different aspects of television production which has burgeoned since the economic crisis of the late 1990s. The topics range from popular Indonesian music programmes, through imported genres like talent quests, real-life crime and supernatural reality TV, to travel programmes which represent Indonesia to Indonesians through foreign eyes. The articles all give a sense of the energy, vitality and openness of mass television broadcasting formats, although these are usually portrayed in the mass communications and media studies' literature as either effectively determined by multinational corporations or else conventional to the point of sterility. As a collection, these pieces, with their stress on television as complex sets of situated practices, offer new ways of approaching one of Asia's major media industries.

Before going any further, it is perhaps worth pausing for a moment to consider some of the reasons for devoting a special issue of the *Asian Journal of Communication* to Indonesian popular entertainment television. Of the larger Asian countries, Indonesia is among the least represented in English-language publications. Major collections claiming to offer coherent coverage of non-Western or Asian media routinely not only exclude Indonesia—the third most populous Asian country—but they fail even to remark on this omission (for example, Curran & Park, 2000; Erni & Chua, 2005, respectively). The reasons are several. Part pertains to academic fashion, which in turn often rides on the coattails of political and economic priorities. So Asia easily becomes reducible to high-profile countries, usually India, China, Japan or possibly Korea. Part is to do with how many Asian scholars from different countries have received training in the West, and so command the codes for acceptance by international English-language publications. Part is also due to the relative paucity, until recently, of Western scholars working on Indonesian media.[1] Specific historical and cultural considerations also come into play. Indonesia's often rumbustious political history and repressive attitude toward intellectuals has not always been clement to research and publication. Perhaps this is why Singapore, the home of the *Asian Journal of Communication*, has long felt uneasy about its vast neighbour and so has often proceeded as if it did not really exist. It is my hope that this collection will help stimulate interest among scholars of Asian media.

There are, of course, also more positive reasons for discussing contemporary Indonesian mass media. Television has been inseparable from the project of national development ever since Indonesia was one of the first countries to launch a civilian satellite, Palapa, in 1976 and to place a television set (car-battery-powered where necessary) in every village. The aim was to reach out across the vast and sprawling archipelago and to address—or *interpellate* in Althusserian terms (1984)—the population, first as the masses or as citizens-in-development and then, with the emergence of terrestrial and satellite commercial television in the 1990s, in various more differentiated ways, including notably as consumers (Kitley, 2000). Television was also vital in the New Order's articulation of political, ethnic and other differences as 'culture', with each geographical region being identified by its distinctive dress styles, performing and plastic arts, and so forth. However, television, together with radio and the Internet, was also key to the downfall of President Suharto in 1998 (Sen & Hill, 2000). The abolition of the Ministry of Information and the relaxation of state censorship under Suharto's successor, Habibie, ushered in a period of dynamism and expansion of media in general, and of television in particular.

Although print media, together with largely decentralized and sometimes radical radio, are important for understanding contemporary Indonesia, it is television which preoccupies the Indonesian political classes and which most viewers consider their main source of information. However, television audiences, reared on the propaganda of the New Order régime, and familiar with the rhetorical devices of local popular theatre and literature, are often remarkably skilled at the critical interpretation of broadcasting.

In order to attract advertising revenue and to fill broadcasting time, most television comprises what one might broadly call entertainment. Accurate figures are not available,[2] but it is generally assumed that most of the population of some 250 million can access and watch television. So the Indonesian market is potentially large. However, it is differentiated in cross-cutting ways by age, class, ethnicity, political affiliation and religion.[3] So the search by the commercial channels for formats which will attract such a heterogeneous viewing population, which now tends quickly to tire of the latest fashion, leads at once to experimentation and adaptation of foreign genres, and to the unabashed imitation of locally successful programmes until audiences get bored. State television, which is still subject to various government guidelines on content, languishes accordingly. For the last 30 years, television has been inextricably intertwined with nation-building and with attempts to create an embracing and hegemonic vision of a single people, sharing a kaleidoscopic culture from Sabang in Aceh to Merauke in West Papua. To study television is to study how Indonesians have been invited to imagine themselves and others.

Culturalist Approaches to Indonesian Media

As the stress upon how Indonesians engage with television suggests, this collection adopts a broadly culturalist approach. Although they come from different disciplinary backgrounds—cultural anthropology, critical cultural and media studies, ethnomusicology and religious studies—as specialists in different aspects of Indonesia, the contributors all recognize how distinctive cultural understandings affect Indonesian programme production, distribution and reception. Certain processes of broadcasting—as an industry—are obviously similar to other Asian countries. However, the same cannot necessarily be said for its broader social implications and how they are discussed publicly, as well as the inflection of the programming itself and how it is implicated in viewers' lives. The latter are far more distinct to Indonesia. Political-economic or mass communications approaches to television, for instance, would have difficulty addressing the cultural factors which determine programming content (Barkin), how imported talent contests engage audiences (Coutas), the penchant for supernatural reality TV (Hobart), still less the success of local *dangdut* music as a challenge to contemporary pop music (Weintraub).

   This collection, however, is not primarily concerned with the long-running debate as to the relative merits of quantitative as against qualitative approaches in media studies. Indeed the terms of this debate may well be misconceived (Hobart, 2006, p. 499). Our concern is more constructive. It is to show how culturally sensitive analyses can enrich media and communications studies. Such an approach has wider ethical and political implications. Political-economic and mass communications schools take it for granted that the theories and methods developed in European and American universities are sufficient effectively to explain relevant media and communications processes without reference to the practices and understandings of producers, audiences and commentators—here Indonesians. As Asians become major world producers of film and television, new styles of production, working practices, aesthetics and commentary by media professionals and intellectuals on film and media themselves have emerged, which require recognition if we are genuinely to address the implications of the postcolonial critique.

Why Entertainment Television?

Entertainment television is often considered frivolous and not worth study except as evidence of global media trends and how ideology is inculcated through popular programming.[4] If we are to understand the political, social and cultural significance of television, surely we should be looking at serious genres, like news, current affairs, documentaries, political talk shows and development broadcasting. Is it not there that the nation is on display and opinion is formed and promulgated? This argument however is inadequate, because it rests upon questionable presuppositions about how media work, a consideration of which involves critical media theory.

Several issues are of immediate relevance. Media and communications studies often ignore the fact that production and reception are not timeless activities, but have histories. Most accounts also presume that the meaning intended by the producers approximates what viewers understand. Not only does the evidence from ethnographic studies of viewers suggest otherwise, but the transmission model of communication is theoretically problematic in itself. These accounts involve unacknowledged assumptions about human nature and rationality. They also assume that objective processes are independent of the practices which constitute them and the situations in which they take place. Finally, academics tend to give weight to issues and practices that are central to their own lives. So they focus on 'serious' programming as 'text'—consider the strange metaphor of 'reading' television. And they have difficulty imagining how other people—most notably 'the masses'—might have quite different ideas and practices (Baudrillard, 1983).

Television viewing involves distinctive histories of practices and cultural understandings. After over 20 years of the state broadcasting rigidly controlled, highly conventionalized, anodyne and often evidently counter-factual or manipulated news and documentary (Kitley, 2000)—even by the standards of these highly formalized genres—audiences have become largely sceptical and critical. Current affairs and documentary are not a good route to understanding how people imagine and talk about themselves if they are widely dismissed by viewers.[5] In the heady days following Suharto's resignation, political talk shows (which were conveniently cheap to broadcast) flourished as different scenarios of reform were aired. Three years later, as the problems of overturning long-entrenched networks of power and collusion became apparent, such programmes had all but disappeared. Indeed 'serious' news was being cut back in favour of more sensational fare like crime and the doings of celebrities.

The assumption that serious or factual broadcasting is received seriously or factually presupposes some kind of equivalence, the preservation of essential meaning, between what the producers imagine programming to be about and how audiences in fact interpret and make use of what they watch. This myth is a necessary fiction of political communication. But it does not follow that media and communications specialists should concur. The conventional argument that underpins the consonance of meaning for producers and receivers is some version of the transmission model. This states that senders transmit messages which are received relatively intact by receivers; and potential miscommunication can be eliminated by repetition. The argument is as beguilingly appealing as it is wrong. For a start, the proponents of the strong version, the mathematical theory of communication, explicitly warned against applying their model to social communication. Referring to the semantic problems of communication, that is the relation of how senders interpret messages as against receivers, Shannon warned that this is a very deep and involved situation, even when one deals only with the relatively simpler problems of communicating through speech (Shannon & Weaver, 1949).

In one of the founding texts of media studies, Stuart Hall (1980) argued against assuming the isomorphism of encoding and decoding television, on the grounds that to do so ignored the relations of production and reception involved. However, the difficulties of knowing how audiences engage with the mass media are far more intractable than even Hall allowed, as his critique retains aspects of the presuppositions he sets out to question (Hobart, 2006).

Transmission models anticipate how large and heterogeneous populations engage with the mass media and so make all sorts of presuppositions about human nature. The risk is evident that élites, including academics, project onto the viewing public either a vision of how they imagine themselves or else the public as somehow lacking. What distinguishes Indonesian television producers, as Barkin notes, is precisely that their backgrounds are quite different from their viewers'. So either television functions to bridge the gap—to mediate—between inadequate humanity and how they should ideally be, or television gives them what suits the executives. However, the viewing masses are also prone to being misled, which is why entertainment media engender such an equivocal reaction among academics and political élites.[6]

Two other sets of presuppositions are also widely implicated in mass communications approaches. The first takes it as unproblematic that media content is adequately described as texts containing messages which are—or should be—in what Basil Bernstein designated the 'elaborated code' used by the middle classes and ultimately propositional. As television is strongly visual and auditory, quite how images and music, which are so central to entertainment media, are supposed to work is far less clear. The second is about rationality. There is confusion as to whether the notion of reason in analyses of the mass media is descriptive (describes what is the case), prescriptive (states what should be the case) or formal (outlines the conditions of intelligibility). Development media conventionally stress the second. The aim is to communicate the desirability of modernity to be achieved through rational development. It follows neither that how people engage with television can adequately be described using rationality nor that formal conditions are sufficient to delineate how media are understood and used.

By contrast the contributors here are interested in the diversity of both producers and viewers, and in the variety of media-related practices which occur. Their concern is how both producers and viewers are differentiated by class, gender, ethnicity, age and other factors. They do not assume some pre-social homunculus which is the essential transmitter and recipient of the media (Henriquez, Hollway, Urwin, Venn, & Walkerdine, 1984). Instead, the contributors work against a background of the practices of production (designing formats, meeting deadlines, positioning themselves within the industry) and readers' and viewers' practices (watching, reading, interpreting, commenting, and engaging or refusing to engage in different situations).

Another problem involves preconceptions, partly shared it seems, by both the political classes and academics. Put simply, they tend to assume that, because something is important and serious to them, *ipso facto* it is to the rest of the population. Ideally programme content should inform and instruct. Although they may not be particularly interested, people ought to take politics and current affairs seriously. (What the viewing public actually do tune in and watch is the theme of several contributions here.) It is far from clear though that the realism implicit in such accounts adequately represents how the mass media work. Summing up research on news broadcasts, Fiske (1989, p. 308) noted how news and current affairs are structured according to such highly conventional narrative codes that we are 'justified in thinking of the news as masculine soap opera'.

The key word here is 'serious', the antitheses of which are 'frivolous' or 'entertaining'—the resonances of the dichotomy deriving, as Dyer has noted, from the distinction between labour and leisure. Entertainment rejects the claims of morality, politics and aesthetics in a culture which still accords these high status. It is born of a society that both considers leisure and pleasure to be secondary and even inferior to the businesses of producing and reproducing, work and family, and yet invests much energy, desire and money into promoting them (Dyer, 1992a, p. 2).

> In a functional analysis, leisure can be seen either as a way of compensating for the dreariness of work or else as the passivity attendant on industrial labour ... But the richness and variety of actual forms of leisure suggest that leisure should also be seen as the creation of meaning in a world in which work and the daily round are characterized by drudgery, insistence and meaninglessness. (Dyer, 1992b, p. 13)

Dyer's argument points to how the value-laden dichotomy between serious media and entertainment involves unacknowledged presuppositions about class interests in capitalist societies. It also offers a way out of the commonsensical idea that entertainment for the masses worldwide is adequately explained by recourse to an uncritical appeal to 'escapism'. Morson (1995) has noted an unappreciated alternative to the narrative technique of foreshadowing. This is a device widely used in literature and media, in which future events are anticipated, so giving the narrative a sense of completeness and finality, which stands however in stark antithesis to lived experience. This alternative he designated as 'sideshadowing', which is the recognition that at each point in our lives there are many alternative possibilities, most of which remain unactualized. These sideshadows constitute the repertoire of narrative and, for viewers, the appreciation of other possibilities in human lives and their ineradicable openness. Entertainment—even pop song contests—arguably involves sideshadowing.[7]

The Argument

Taken together, the articles in this collection offer an argument for the critical examination of the cultural practices which constitute Indonesian entertainment television. Gareth Barkin's piece demonstrates the contribution anthropology can make to understanding processes of production. Drawing upon his ethnography of production houses and channels in Jakarta, he shows how the format, content and style of programming depend on issues of 'intra-group prestige' and 'the internal, aesthetic politics of Jakarta's "culture of production" and the sorts of forms, narratives and themes that resonate within it'. Starting with a pilot travel programme for TransTV, he examines how decisions have little to do with anticipating audience demand or interest, but reflect executives' overseas education and their distinctively élite tastes affected by global media narratives. The result is that, in travel and many other genres, the subject position presented to viewers is often foreign. So Indonesian viewers are invited to adopt a 'foreignizing gaze' upon themselves, reified in travel programmes as exotic and commoditized 'culture'. Barkin's article suggests the importance of ethnographic analyses of media production to complement political-economic studies.

The other three articles examine issues around the popularity of the highest-rated genres of programmes over the last few years: interactive singer-performer talent quests, crime and supernatural reality TV, and local *dangdut* music. Penny Coutas examines Indonesian imports of global brands, notably the tightly-regulated *Idol* format. She considers whether these support the cultural imperialism thesis, voiced in the Indonesian press, which argues that multinational corporations dominate high-profile media production in developing countries. On audiences, Coutas notes that 'in many respects ... the real "consumers" of *Indonesian Idol* are the advertisers themselves, whilst "the audience" ... constitute the product'. And *Idola Indonesia* presents the West as 'the "ideal" and participation in a global network of celebrity as being the ultimate accomplishment in the entertainment world'. However, she notes there is much that economic and quantitative analyses cannot explain, from the cultural role of interactivity to the heterogeneity of audiences or how programmes are 'glocalized'. Coutas distinguishes ordinary viewers, who rarely vote, from supporters (*pendukung*) who participate actively and wield a degree of agency. Whatever the global parameters, Indonesian audiences use such programmes imaginatively to re-think Indonesia, its place in the world and their own lives.

In my article, I examine two genres of reality TV, which have attracted high ratings and extensive criticism in the press from intellectuals and the political élite, namely, real-life crime and supernatural reality programmes. These genres stand opposed to the disproportionate—and largely fantastic—representation of the upper middle classes in being about 'ordinary people'. An analysis of the broadsheet debates, however, reiterates the gulf that Barkin also highlights between the Indonesian élite and the majority of the population. I consider whether these genres are conservative in that narratively they reassert social order against threats, or might constitute sites of potential resistance. As audiences come to television with cultural pre-understandings from Indonesian popular theatre and literature, I argue that such programmes open up possibilities undreamed of in cultural and media studies.

Andrew Weintraub explores the broadcasting history of popular hybrid music, *dangdut*. *Dangdut* was 'associated with urban underclass audiences' and depicted in popular print media as 'backward, hickish, and unsophisticated'. As new recording and broadcasting technologies disseminated *dangdut*, intellectuals represented it by contrast to Western pop not only as the music of Indonesians, but also through *dangdut* '"the people" could be harnessed for their sheer numbers in imagining a national culture'. In so doing, however, the masses 'receded even further from representation'. Beyond official enunciations about the masses, 'however, lies the wild exuberance and pleasure of *dangdut*', moments where the antagonisms of nostalgia for the past and rampant commercialism, between classes, and of political representation are worked out. So popular music, the raucous epitome of entertainment, emerges as perhaps more revelatory than are the texts of the political and intellectual élite about the intricate discourse in which Indonesians participate about the conditions of their lives and futures through the mass media.

Acknowledgements

The editors and contributors offer their special thanks to Philip Kitley, who reviewed the draft articles for publication. Philip's contribution went well beyond the usual task of a referee and he made invaluable suggestions on all the articles, which have significantly improved the collection as a whole. We would also like to acknowledge the helpfulness and unflagging support of Professors Eddie Kuo and Ben Detenber of AJC. We additionally wish to thank both the Association of Asian Studies and the Indonesian and East Timor Studies Committee for their generous financial support for a panel on Indonesian entertainment media at the 2005 annual meetings in Chicago at which earlier drafts of these papers were first presented for discussion. Finally, we would like to acknowledge the contribution of our discussant at that panel, Dr Faruk ht, of Universitas Gadjah Mada.

Notes

[1] Among the notable exceptions are David Hill, Philip Kitley and Krishna Sen. Fortunately there is now a generation of young scholars working on aspects of Indonesian media, some of whom are represented in this collection.

[2] An ACNielsen survey of nine major cities in 2005 showed over 92% of people watched television.

[3] The number of major 'cultures' and languages in Indonesia varies depending on how one defines and differentiates between them. Most estimates exceed at least 300.

[4] Popular culture constitutes an 'arena of consent and resistance ... where hegemony arises, and where it is secured ... [It is] one of the places where socialism might be constituted. That is why "popular culture" matters ... Otherwise, to tell you the truth, I don't give a damn about it' (Hall, 1981, pp. 230–231, 239). However, the arguments about popular culture as an object of study are not immediately relevant here and have been rehearsed elsewhere (for example, Fiske, 1989; McGuigan, 1992).

[5] The notable exception to this, at least between 2003 and 2005 when I studied local television stations in Java and Bali, was local news, which achieved the highest programme ratings (although television executives privately doubted their accuracy). A key reason seems to be that local news is fairly easily corroborated independently and so viewers learn how to incorporate stations' biases.

[6] There is an implicit Christian imagery of humanity as fallen. However, other religions and political doctrines have alternative ways of constituting the masses as lacking.

[7] Unfortunately, because of publication deadlines, we were not able to include an intriguing piece in preparation by Faruk from Universitas Gadjah Mada on the top-rated sitcom *Bajaj Bajuri*, set among the Jakarta underclass. *Bajaj Bajuri* creates worlds of possibility through a complex play of realism and aspiration. From the analysis of viewers' commentaries, Faruk shows how viewers are reflexively aware that they are watching a genre historically positioned in relation to previous genres. He also explicates how a popular comedy offers a subtle commentary on representations of both class and realism in the Indonesian mass media.

References

Althusser, L. (1984). Ideology and ideological state apparatuses. In *Essays on ideology*. London: Verso.

Baudrillard, J. (1983). *In the shadow of the silent majorities . . . or the end of the social and other essays* (P. Foss, P. Patton, & J. Johnston, Trans.). New York: Semiotext(e).

Curran, J., & Park, M-J. (Eds.). (2000). *Dewesternizing media studies*. London & New York: Routledge.

Dyer, R. (1992a). Introduction. In *Only entertainment*. London: Routledge.

Dyer, R. (1992b). The notion of entertainment. In *Only entertainment*. London: Routledge.

Erni, J. N., & Chua, S. K. (2005). *Asian media studies: Politics of subjectivities*. Oxford: Blackwell.

Fiske, J. (1989). *Television culture*. London: Routledge.

Hall, S. (1980). Encoding/decoding. In S. Hall, D. Hobson, A. Lowe, & P. Willis (Eds.), *Culture, media, language: Working papers in cultural studies, 1972–79*. London: Unwin Hyman.

Hall, S. (1981). Notes on deconstructing 'the popular'. In R. Samuel (Ed.), *People's history and socialist theory*. London: Routledge & Kegan Paul.

Henriques, J., Hollway, W., Urwin, C., Venn, C., & Walkerdine, V. (1984). *Changing the subject: Psychology, social regulation and subjectivity*. London: Methuen.

Hobart, M. (2006). Just talk? Anthropological reflections on the object of media studies in Indonesia. *Asian Journal of Social Science*, 34(3), 492–519.

Kitley, P. (2000). *Television, nation, and culture in Indonesia*. Athens, Ohio: University Center for International Studies.

McGuigan, J. (1992). *Cultural populism*. London: Routledge.

Morson, G. S. (1995). *Narrative and freedom: The shadows of time*. New Haven, CT: Yale University Press.

Sen, K., & &. Hill, D. T. (2000). *Media, culture, and politics in Indonesia*. South Melbourne: Oxford University Press.

Shannon, C., & Weaver, W. (Eds.). (1949). *The mathematical theory of communication*. Urbana, IL: University of Illinois Press.

The Foreignizing Gaze: Producers, Audiences, and Symbols of the 'Traditional'

Gareth Barkin

Indonesian television production relies greatly on *media narratives* and forms, linked in popular constellations and disembedded from those global sources that comprise the broad mediascape accessible to producers and programmers (Barkin, 2004).[1] In this article, I will focus on a particular case study—the pilot episode of a travel program that was aired at TransTV's first broadcast—in an effort to demonstrate how derived form and narrative can be selectively and creatively incorporated into local programs, and the resultant shifts in popular meaning and audience subjectivity. I will argue further that the 'culture of production' and its orientation toward intra-group prestige, which differentially permeates areas of the production environment, contributes to the use of particular media narratives and forms for purposes that transform their semiotics in unexpected ways. The primary finding of this article, which is contextualized from the case study to other areas of Indonesian television, is that producers' heavy reliance on global media narratives, combined with the community emphasis on certain forms of prestige, has led to content that positions local audiences as foreigners when 'gazing' toward regional Indonesian cultures and markers of tradition. This *foreignizing gaze*, most easily observed in travel and labeled 'lifestyle programming', is latent across a large spectrum of the Indonesian mediascape and has its basis in the histories, tensions and exigencies of Jakarta's production culture, fueled by multinational corporate sponsorship.[2]

Research for this article was conducted from January 2001 to July 2002 among Indonesia's television producers and broadcasters, extended later via conversations and correspondence with informants within and outside the industry. Building from the work of Ang (1991, 1996) and Appadurai (1991, 1996), my goal in this project was to investigate ideologies and practices behind the influential models of national culture and lifestyle produced by private television companies; how and why they imagine and target particular audience demographics; and how they integrate conflicting and sensitive social issues into commercially successful media.

TransTV's Premiere

TransTV President Ishadi SK had used his connections with government network TVRI to allow his new station—largely staffed by recent college graduates with little or no experience in the industry—to use its facilities for training purposes. A key training goal was to execute a 'trial broadcast' of several hours to be broadcast over a local transmitter, so that anyone in the immediate Yogyakarta region could conceivably tune it in. Since most people do not spend time scanning their television dial for newly appearing stations, however, it was clear that the event was largely meant for audiences other than the central Javanese public, and that the transmission element was largely ceremonial. The first of these audiences were the station's investors who wanted some tangible proof that the station was moving along on schedule and would be capable of beginning real 'nation-wide' broadcasts later that year. The second included various 'VIP's' who had been invited to attend the screening. These ranged from competitors in commercial television, to politicians and journalists. A great deal was at stake in impressing these groups who would largely generate the 'buzz' surrounding TransTV, for better or worse, when they all returned to Jakarta.

The broadcast featured a combination of live and taped content in an effort to demonstrate both that the station was capable of producing high quality narrative programming with excellent production values, as well as adequately control all the variables needed to produce a live show or news feed. Indeed the showpiece of the broadcast was a music and variety program, which was broadcast live and with few technical mistakes, to the relief of all involved. Live news segments, complete with 'on the scene' reporters, were also successfully executed, although the news programs did tend to rely more heavily on pre-taped 'human interest' segments. Even mock commercials were broadcast in order to more closely approximate real-world conditions.

Anak Muda Punya Mau

The most interesting part of the broadcast for me, however, was a half-hour, youth-oriented travel program called *Anak Muda Punya Mau*. The title, which uses non-standard Indonesian, might literally translate as 'Young kids have desires', but might also be translated as 'Young kids want to go'. The program centered on a young, attractive female host, who was shown bounding around touristy areas in Yogyakarta, one of Indonesia's more popular tourist destinations, and a city which is commonly described in travel books as the 'cultural heart' of Indonesia. The scenes of the host walking down the street or making her way through tourist areas were presented in a style reminiscent of early MTV. Extreme angles were used, and the film was sped up.

These segments, however, came quickly to an end when the host reached a point of interest. The music faded to the distant background, and the host addressed the camera directly with scripted comments about where she was and what she was doing. In one of these segments, she was on Malioboro Street, a boulevard of Yogyakarta well known for its craft and 'antique' shops as well as sidewalks packed with vendors selling wood carvings, Javanese shadow puppets, leather goods and various other crafts, most of which are locally produced.

The host stopped at a shop selling *wayang kulit* (leather shadow puppets), and went in for a quick lesson in how they were made. The shopkeeper and puppet maker was an elderly Javanese man dressed in 'traditional' clothing, including a batik kain. While he offered a brief explanation of the different types of shadow puppets and how they were made, the camera movement and the background music changed. Extreme close-ups were used on the man's face and hands, while classical Javanese gamelan music came up in the background. The camera also performed slow tracking shots. The tone of the segment had shifted radically from a fast-paced, MTV style to a slower if equally slick mode reminiscent of certain Hollywood genre films and TV programs that romanticize the 'primitive' as a vessel of sacred wisdom (Lutz & Collins, 1993).

What Was That All About?

This pilot episode provides a unique window into the internal, aesthetic politics of Jakarta's 'culture of production' and the sorts of forms, narratives and themes that resonate within it. Without the skewing pressures of targeting particular audience demographics within a particular programming context, the program's producers were free to create what they thought would be most impressive to people like themselves. Although this sort of goal may always be on the agenda for most producers, rarely is it allowed the sort of time and financing given *Anak Muda*. While the program may not be considered an entirely typical example of its genre—as manifest on Indonesian national programming schedules—it was prototypical in the sense that it exhibited an ideal style from which dilution and reorientation, in various directions and for various reasons, would be required in a conventional production environment. As one producer commented, 'That is the sort of travel show we need to be making ... that is the sort of travel show I'd like to make' (personal communication, 18 February 2002).[3]

There are a number of important factors in understanding the larger context surrounding the choices made in this particular production. One inescapable fact that forms the principal backdrop to this project is that Indonesian television producers tend to come from backgrounds that are radically different than most of their audiences. Many of them are foreign-born, have international backgrounds, either national or ethnic/linguistic, or have spent a great deal of time abroad. Spending time abroad, in fact, appeared to be an important prerequisite for success in the industry, less because it may allow the acquisition of specific expertise in some industry-related skill, than through the status it bought within the top-tier crowd of station executives and leading producers, as well as the blunt prestige it bought among those in the industry who had not had the opportunity to travel.

Nowhere in the television lineup is the disparity between worldviews of producers and audiences more starkly apparent than in the travel program. This is not only visible in the particulars of such programs' lifestyle messages, but most dramatically in the very notion of producing a vacation-oriented travel show to begin with, in a country where recent figures show 27.1% of the population is below the United Nations poverty line (United Nations, 2003).

'Lifestyle shows' or 'light entertainment programming'—such as travel programs—were, however, the most important new market on the Indonesian television scene during the time of my fieldwork. This was partially because their ratings were on the rise, but largely because they—like the much lamented 'reality programs' of the United States—are far less expensive to produce than are conventional narrative genres, including the *sinetron*. In the case of the programs produced by one expatriate American producer, costs were further reduced by the heavy use of imported footage, which he 're-packaged' with Indonesian announcers and cut-scenes, for domestic broadcast—a common practice on the often overlooked range of production possibilities that exist between 'purely' foreign or domestic programs. ACNielsen (1993–2003, 2002, 2004) partially confirmed the trending predictions I had heard from producers, though comparisons were difficult because the agency does not label these sorts of programs as a distinct genre, and because many programs are produced only in short runs.

Anak Muda was typical of the genre in that it incorporated a fascinating variety of narrative and formal elements lifted from transnational media sources. Most interesting was the issue of how meanings and expression shifted when these elements were taken and used in the context of an Indonesian commercial program. For example, a host of a certain age and gender, dressing and behaving a certain way in a certain context, using certain language and expressions, may invoke a range of widely (if imperfectly) shared meanings in American or British audiences who see her on a National Geographic or BBC travel program. However, the same formal and narrative elements, disembeded and reconstructed as part of an Indonesian program, may invoke an entirely different group of meanings; certainly, producers appear to intend it to. Further, the lack of a shared media-cultural history with such forms and narratives may reduce the likelihood of shared meanings among audiences, yielding a more confusing or incoherent program. It is precisely this semiotic shift which accompanies the use of foreign media narratives by producers in Indonesia. It emerged as the central theme of this project because I found this practice to be neither haphazard nor artless, but instead a sophisticated calculation of nationally shared (if still emergent) symbolic codes.

While lifting many narratives directly from other media sources, one of the less visible imports is the program's embedded, preferential positioning of the audience (see Abu-Lughod, 1997, 2002). Although there are many potential assumptions about the audience that may be encoded in borrowed forms and narratives, the most prominent in *Anak Muda* was that it appeared to position the viewer squarely as a foreigner. By introducing various aspects of 'traditional' culture in very much the same way as it might to a Western spectator in a program about foreign travel, the program positions audiences as foreign to Javanese culture, foreign to Indonesian history, and foreign to 'local' customs and lifestyles generally. These 'foreign' aspects of culture, in turn, were represented romantically, as moderately interesting and certainly exotic, but ultimately not to be taken seriously beyond a context of cultural consumption. Indeed the host was shopping throughout the program, buying souvenirs and trinkets to take back to her culturally disconnected, modern world; presumably based in the high rises of Jakarta. But rather than an intentional use of foreign media forms and narratives for the purpose of invoking domestically particular meanings in audiences, this foreign positioning appeared to be an inadvertent by-product of the process.

In speaking with Sutoyo, one of the program's producers, weeks after the broadcast, I raised the issue of foreignization. He did not appear particularly interested in talking about the subject *per se*, but rather framed his responses in terms of his skill at identifying and incorporating new and prestigious constellations of narrative and form into the program.

> I am not in charge of the talking, the script—other people do that. I decided what [the show] would look like, where [the host] would go and what she would do, and I chose her as well. I did the casting. I watch many programs of this type in my travels abroad, and I know what will work with the Indonesian people. This way I could also show the bigwigs [at the premiere] that we understand the trends in global television, that we are not going to be like, you know, another TPI. We know the latest trends. (Sutoyo, personal communication, 6 April 2001)

Connection to *Anak Muda*?

Communications models for 'Third World national cinemas' leave an awkward legacy for a study of cultural self-representation. Focused on political speech, rather than broader cultural themes, models such as Teshome Gabriel's (1985) 'three phase' development structure posits a brief and unilinear progression from (1) imitation of Hollywood, to (2) use of 'traditional' forms and narrative, which are appropriated from other sorts of cultural products, to (3) the final phase in which 'traditional cultures' are examined critically by the filmmaker. Krishna Sen (1994, p. 46), in applying this model to early Indonesian cinema, finds it more useful when we 'think of Gabriel's phases as competing patterns of film-making, rather than historical periods that follow one another'. Nevertheless, the problems in applying this model go beyond its linear structure, as it posits that developing nations must always be responding to or rejecting Hollywood, and frames the moral content of this struggle as one in which derivation is a synonym for underdevelopment and subservience. The focus on examination of 'traditional cultures' in the model's later phases appears well intentioned, but obscures the possibility of low-derivation filmmaking (Gabriel's apparent measure of both quality and liberty) in the developing world that deals with issues such as modernity, transnationalism, foreign cultures, and a long list of other topics that do not relate directly to historic cultural traditions—nor discourses of 'the traditional'—within the producing region.

TransTV's *Anak Muda* makes for a particularly poignant case study because it combines the sorts of cultural models that have resulted from the industry's escalating emphasis on material wealth and prestige—seen in *sinetron* and else-where—with a 'traditional' Indonesian setting in the form of a domestic travel destination. It is in programs like this that we can see just how far Jakarta's culture of production has grown away from the consumers of its products, and how this disparity can be fed back to spectators, giving them the producer's 'way of looking' (see Mulvey, 1975/1988, 1989), allowing them to enjoy vicariously a foreign, cosmopolitan, and sometimes condescending perspective on people with whom they likely share far more than they do with Jakarta's media élite.

Western academics and journalists' initial reaction to such programs is that they are 'rip offs', and somehow unbefitting Indonesian audiences (field notes, 3 February 2001, 12 March 2001, 9 September 2001). Indeed this appears to be the visceral basis of Gabriel's scale: a discourse that appeals to notions of common sense and postcolonialism, and that posits mass media in developing countries as morally obligated to represent local culture above all. To illustrate the process of intentional derivation, and to demonstrate why it might best be understood outside such a value-laden framework, I will show how the producers of *Anak Muda* selectively appropriated and recombined elements from disparate sources to come up with a program that—although drawing on many global media sources—evidences a locally particular style grounded in Jakarta's culture of production. In order to do this, I will (a) present a list of various narrative conventions (and related formal elements) common to Western travel programs—*Anak Muda*'s primary source—and then (b) discuss which of these constellations were chosen, which were chosen from other sources, and how they were negotiated and transformed during the local production process. These insights are drawn from an extensive review of foreign travel programs available in Indonesia,[4] largely through satellite broadcasts, as well as interviews with producers of Indonesian travel and light entertainment programs.

Western Media-Bound Travel Narratives

These Western travel programs tend to follow a single narrator, often female, as she makes her way to one or several tourist destinations, showing viewers her experiences from the perspective of a traveling companion, while offering them information about such perennial travel topics as food, accommodation, points of interest, and of course the more amorphous 'culture', as in the phrase 'If you'd like to take in some local culture . . . ' An implicit presumption of such programs is that the viewer will be able to make use of the information in a practical manner. The information on different hotel options, for example, would not seem to serve any explicit entertainment purpose for a viewer who had no interest or intention to travel to the particular destination (though see the next section for a discussion of how it may, in the case of Indonesian travel programs). It would, however, function as a practical video guidebook for the viewer open to considering such a trip, and who is able to afford one.

The manner in which these programs represent the people and cultures that they are profiling certainly merits a discussion of its own, but for our purposes, two critical points will suffice. First, these programs encode a strong doctrine of cultural relativity, in that there is no judgment or relative valuation of a given area's 'culture'; the perspective is somewhat reminiscent of the early Boazian concept of culture. Particularly on the BBC, where these programs are most common, they demonstrate an undercurrent of political liberalism and reflexivity, albeit often superficial and uninformed. They follow in the tradition of student-oriented travel guides that, while they are marketed as politically progressive, have been shown to reinforce structures of power and exacerbate wealth disparities in the regions they cover (Laderman, 2002; White & White, 2004). Indeed, Lonely Planet, one of the most popular publishers of such guides, now produces its own television series that is sold as a syndication package to buyers such as National Geographic Channel or other transnational broadcasters. One possible function of this orientation seems to be the alleviation of inchoate guilt, on the part of the viewer, at potentially exploiting former colonial subjects (Bhabha, 1992).

Second, travel programs such as those on the BBC create a representation of local culture that focuses, predictably, on those elements that vacationing Westerners are reasonably expected to consume. This leads to representations restricted both by time—vacationers are assumed to have only a short time to spend in any given locale—and by various qualitative factors that producers consider appropriate guidelines for the conservative model of traveler they wish to create. For example, a travel program will not demonstrate how to get a job in a particular destination, because such an act would be well out of the popularly held norm for holiday/travel behavior. Likewise, such programs will not instruct travelers as to where they might buy illicit drugs or hire a prostitute.[5] Such behaviors do fall within the agendas of some travelers, particularly to mainland Southeast Asia, but they are presumably outside the moral envelope of a light entertainment show. What come to the fore, then, are cultural forms that can be quickly and easily consumed, and that demonstrate a high level of exoticism so as to create a compelling difference between the viewer's own local experience and the destination being profiled (see Furisch, 2002).

Encoded in these foci are numerous cultural norms that loosely fit with producers' imagined audiences, including their backgrounds, their interests and desires, their limitations and prejudices. Among those foreign travel programs available in Indonesia, I have compiled the following list of implicit norms that are broadly present and frequently reinterpreted by producers in Indonesia.

Two Weeks' Vacation

> How much time will the person have in this place? Should we plan on a weekend trip, or could it be weeks and weeks? (Andi, travel show producer, production meeting, 12 February 2002)

This target range is evidenced frequently in hosts' comments regarding what can be 'done' in a particular amount of time, with the presumption that, having traveled a presumably great distance, one would likely have at least two weeks to spend there. Often additional sub-trips or nearby destinations are noted for the traveler who has more time. The more backpacker-oriented programs tend to presume a greater amount of available time, and also tend to focus more on a tour of multiple locations within a given region than the 'vacation' model.

Producers I spoke with paid only cursory attention to this issue. 'Most Indonesians don't take vacations like this [as depicted on the show] anyway', Andi told me, 'so we assume maybe it's a business traveler or who knows?' (personal communication, 9 March 2002). I got the sense that producers were not putting themselves in the shoes of a potential viewer who took the show for what it functionally purported to be. They were interested in emulating certain aesthetic and narrative aspects of foreign programs, but did not concern themselves with the internal logic of such shows. This was evidenced by frequent discussions of what 'travel show styles' to incorporate, and only rare conversations about issues that might concern a traveler. To the extent that certain implicit assumptions regarding the length of the trip moved into their production, they were likely the result of adopting other, related narrative norms, such as covering three or four restaurants and two or three 'cultural' attractions or performances.

Sufficiently Wealthy to Travel, but Bargain-Seeking

> That restaurant is too cheap, too rural.[6] (Tuti, travel show production assistant, production meeting, 15 November 2001)

Programs are built around the presumption that viewers are able to afford the sort of trip being represented in the show, or something similar. They do not tend to presume great wealth, but rather 'Western' middle-income standards, as evidenced in the recurrent focus on bargain-shopping and accommodation. This is exaggerated in the student-oriented programs, yet the presumption of middle class background, along with liberal cultural politics, remains.

Local producers have an interesting relationship to this theme. On the one hand, they clearly presume an almost infinitely wealthy protagonist, and will shy away from essentially no travel service based on price alone. Here there seems to be a certain amount of pride involved: 'We can do the same things as [foreign tourists] in our own country ... many Indonesians will stay at the Hyatt or the Novotel when they travel; I stay there sometimes', Andi told me (personal communication, 9 March 2002). At the same time, however, bargain-hunting did creep into a number of segments I witnessed being produced. It appeared to be included for what I can only describe as narrative aesthetics; particularly when it came to shopping, the bargain-seeking theme is so prevalent to BBC style travel programs that it was itself regarded as an élite practice, even though, ostensibly, it indicated a limited budget. 'This is the normal style one sees on these shows', said one writer as he was negotiating a passage about the cost of scuba-diving lessons, and whether they should compare different diving centers on the basis of price (field notes, 28 January 2002).

Desire to Explore the Unknown

BBC style travel programs are not simply promotions for relaxing, uneventful vacations. Nor are they geared toward business travelers or others who might wish to avoid local diversity and simply consume goods and services as similar as possible to those with which they are already familiar. Rather, they presume an interest in cultural spectatorship on the part of the audience, as evidenced by the focus on local foods, performance and 'points of interest', as well as their formal style, which often positions the viewer as a compatriot of the host, following her along as she deals with local people and situations, all the while commenting through voice narration, or directly to the camera.

I observed very little of this theme overtly discussed, and it appeared as though the lifestyle model imagined by local producers was not congruous with the intersection of 'adventure' and leisure. Activities were strictly divided into categories such as dining, accommodation, and live performances, but never did I notice anyone express the need to avoid common tourist 'traps', or to look for 'out of the way' destinations or services. In fact, the opposite was true; many were concerned that they would forget to cover one of the most popular restaurants or hotels. The formal/narrative constellation I term 'following the host' was kept in all the productions I observed, however, because 'it helps to create a relationship with the audience ... you need a character, a character to be their friend', said Artono, a writer for a travel show (personal communication, 23 February 2002).

Lack of Relationship to the Destination

It would obviously be near impossible to anticipate viewers' varying relationships to a particular destination—whether they had friends or family who lived there, had visited before, spoke the language, etc. There is instead the presumption of no relationship at all to the destination, as evidenced in the coverage of accommodation options, advice on local language for those who speak none, and the general tenor of the programs' narratives. Interestingly, the hosts of these programs rarely acknowledge any relationship to place either, though as the host of a travel show one might be forgiven for having visited a given destination before. To do so would, however, violate the implicitly surrogate foundation of the relationship between host and viewer, breaking the illusion that the two are exploring a new and exotic locale together.

Although nearly all the productions I observed focused exclusively on domestic, Indonesian travel destinations,[7] they retained this theme in an essentially unmodified fashion. Hosts associate only with colorfully local locals, which is to say locals who embody and impart special knowledge about the destination from the position of 'other'. Never did I see a host look up a friend or relative in a given locale, which might not seem extraordinary if it were not such common practice in Indonesia, including among the producers and crew of these very programs during production. Because language was less of an issue, with everyone speaking Indonesian, producers sometimes took additional steps to exaggerate the cultural distance between host and local (though accents and fluency in formal Indonesian often highlighted this). 'Yes, we tell them to put on traditional clothing, if they're not wearing it, or something to show the local culture', Andi told me of his program, adding 'we want everything to be true/authentic' (field notes, 12 February 2002).

Consumer of Material Culture

> What is there to buy here? (Erik, travel show host, off camera to producers, 18 February 2002)

Though not pervasive, the presumption that viewers will be interested in collecting mementos of their trip is common. In some cases, this can become the focus of a program, as where a particular area is well known for producing a highly consumable commodity, such as a craft or art form with appeal to Western tastes. In more developed destinations, well-known shopping areas may be featured as a point of interest in themselves, such as Singapore's Orchard Road.

This theme is, if anything, exaggerated in local productions. Visits to landmarks and points of interest, such as Borobudur in Central Java, which are not overtly connected to material consumption in any way, are often transformed into shopping excursions, even if the only products available are tourist-market souvenirs. There is a strong emphasis on bringing back 'proof' of the visit—evidence of accomplishment. When I asked one production assistant, Eake, why they always had the host buy something on every trip, she responded, 'If not, when you get home, people would not know you've ever been here' (field notes, 4 March 2002). In *Anak Muda*, consumption acts as a sort of raison d'être for the host's excursions; even history lessons in 'traditional culture' are quickly transformed into consumption when she buys a sack full of *wayang kulit* from the learned Malioboro shopkeeper.

Traveling Alone

Hosts often walk the line between guide and traveling companion of the viewer, sometimes possessing moderate insider knowledge of an area, but also at pains to demonstrate the 'process' of traveling, particularly in the more youth-oriented programs. Dense information and background text is often delivered as a voice-over, rather than by the live host, allowing the viewer to continue to relate to her as someone in a process of discovery.

All the local travel shows I observed used a close variation on this theme. They all had one host, more often female, and often also used a 'following along' style of camera form and direct narration for at least some portions of the shows. Disembodied narration was also common, and always voiced by the host. *Anak Muda* featured a very young, female host, intended to appeal to teenagers (Ishadi, personal communication, 24 October 2002), but in a rather different way than BBC style programs target backpackers; the target teenagers were not necessarily interested in travel, but rather the travel show was just another forum for lifestyle modeling.

Exoticism

As noted above, this is the load-bearing pillar of BBC style travel program narratives, upon which many of the programs' other norms depend. The structure of the programs, designed to find the most interesting elements of local cultures in a very limited time frame, use markers of the exotic to sensationalize common practice. This exotification also distances audience from local subject, dramatizing the sense of 'exploration' noted above. Most importantly, however, the sense of the exotic is relied on as a central reason why audiences might consider a location or 'culture' interesting and worth visiting. Without this sense, the programs would have little ground on which to make their case to viewers, which—particularly when focusing on developing countries—is built around the excitement and adventure of foreign travel.

The adoption of this theme by domestic producers is—it would seem—problematic in the sense that the cultural difference between host/viewer and local subject is not as clear cut as it is for Western programs exploring regions of foreign countries. Producers I spoke with and observed seemed determined to maintain exotic distance, but did not see it as a problem. They did consider themselves as foreigners when they visited many of the shooting locations, and although growing up in Indonesia did reduce the level of exoticism they reportedly felt in response to locals, this only appeared to make them more earnest in exaggerating the exotic on film. It was a barrier to overcome. The vocabulary surrounding this struggle, however, dwelt on words like 'tradition' and 'traditional' (*tradisi/tradisional*), original/authentic (*asli*), and ethic group/tribe (*suku*). Those traditional/authentic elements of local culture that made it to the final cut, however, were invariably the most different and exotic. When I asked cast and crew members of one travel program what their '*suku*' was, many jokingly reported that they did not have one; one production assistant told me 'all of them ... original Jakarta!' (field notes, 28 November 2001).[8]

Visual Aesthetic Reductionism

> How can we make Jakarta look cool? (Andi, travel show producer, production meeting, 12 December 2002)

While scholars might not put much stock in the representations made by travel shows, it should be noted that they have the potential to be received as a voice of authority among audiences through their claims to expert knowledge, which may lead viewers to consider that they are a form of education rather than entertainment (Fursich, 2002). As such, the aesthetic reductionism practiced by their producers, who tend to focus on the most visually compelling elements of cultural life, has the potential to perpetuate a superficial popular discourse about the developing world. This is further evidenced by the moral backdrop against which many of these programs are constructed, which posits a malevolent and accelerating Western cultural hegemony that can be actively opposed by the traveler, who is rewarding and conditioning locals through her consumption of the 'traditional', rather than the modern, demonstrating a sometimes condescending and power-tinged performance of cultural relativism through patronage.

Tito, who was involved in the planning of a new travel show, told me of his producers' obsession with spending a third of each program on local food at the destination. 'You know', he told me, 'some guy from Surabaya already knows what *soto ayam* [a chicken soup] tastes like ... it's available everywhere. All the good Indonesian foods you can get almost anywhere, so what's the point? They want to try to make it look all exotic and delicious, but it's just *soto ayam*' (field notes, 20 March 2002). Tito went on to complain that the producers had a rigid formula in mind, which they had apparently derived from a particular foreign travel program they had seen and admired, and were unwilling to listen to his admonitions regarding the mundanity of Indonesian food to Indonesian audiences. Overall, I witnessed a great focus on visual aesthetics in all the shows I studied, but the BBC style sermonizing was largely absent; 'the traditional' was not represented as under threat or in need of support, but rather as exotic, decontextualized spectacle.

Other Styles

Discussion about forms and styles like this did not come easily to the co-director of *Anak Muda* when I spoke with him. For one thing, he gave the impression that he had little creative freedom, most major decisions having been made by the show's producers. When asked about formal issues such as the use of fast-motion and effects, he noted that it was a common style to use in circumstances where one wants to show a lot of activity quickly, and that the video effects and hard-rock music were part of an effort to orient the show to teenagers. His initial response to such inquiries, however, was to discuss the technology needed to create the effects. He frequently used such phrases as 'we just got this [technology]' or 'we couldn't do this before', indicating in interest in using the latest effects available on the station's limited budget (field notes, 5 August 2001).

Spectrum of Foreignizing Content

While *Anak Muda* makes for a compelling example, the use of potentially foreignizing formal and narrative structures is evident in nearly every corner of Indonesian television production. The forms that have become dominant in the country's most popular genre, the primetime *sinetron*, illustrate how global media influence may flow in a variety of crosscutting directions. For example, the settings of these programs are almost universally large, opulent houses that glitter with gold and marble. These mansions, which often feature a distinctly Indian aesthetic of wealth, are a frequent target of media critics, who criticize stations and production houses for creating unattainable aspirations in a relatively poor country.

Beyond the settings of *sinetron*, there are several issues that foreignize the programs to audiences. The professions of the characters is another issue that is often raised by critics. *Sinetron* characters tend to work in clean, modern office buildings, wearing crisp, professional clothing, yet never is it revealed what their jobs are. The heightened emotionality of performers draws on Latin American *telenovelas*.

Finally, *sinetron* have been accused of glorifying technological modernity and affluence. Producers do indeed often struggle to display the latest models of cell phones on their programs, or have their character driving trendy, new, European luxury cars. These critiques of the *sinetron*, the country's most popular genre, are also often conflated as elements of the argument—voiced by the president and many others—that these programs are simply not reflective of Indonesian national culture, or any widely shared lifestyles or lived cultures in the country.

Foreignizing production practices can be observed in a variety of other program genres as well. From pseudo-historical action shows that use Chinese actors versed in the performance of Hong Kong style filmed martial arts, to 'human interest' segments on the news that romanticize and exotify rural poverty through music, narration and formal choices. The practice I term *cultural bumpering* was also gaining popularity during the period of my fieldwork, and appeared poised to become a powerful formal/narrative convention. This is when the bumpers of a program—the short segments that indicate a transition to or from commercial—display evocative imagery of 'traditional' cultural forms, such as the lead characters wearing clothing associated with an ethnic tradition (but which they rarely, if ever, wear on the show). The practice is not limited to program bumpers either, but is often visible in self-promotional segments aired by the stations themselves. Often the traditional forms are blended with more modern or foreign influences, as when TransTV had a live rock/gamelan orchestra, featuring classical instruments as well as electric guitars and keyboards, to perform bumper material for its variety program. These are meant to 'remind audiences that we are Indonesian, and that we have respect for Indonesian culture', noted Iwan, a programming executive. When I asked him if they would consider featuring such an orchestra, or other 'traditional' cultural performance, during the body of a program he noted, 'Oh no, it's just enough to give them a taste' (personal communication, 28 April 2001).

Discussion

There is a great variety of programming available on commercial television in Indonesia, and it would be irresponsible to argue that all of it positions the viewer as foreign to her own national or regional cultures. Likewise, it would be naïve to suggest that the extent to which many popular programs position audiences in a foreignizing manner is the result of stations' or producers' intentions to do so. Rather, my research suggests a variety of connected factors that, by contributing to the specific economy, politics and culture of television production in Jakarta, have led to the domination of specific discourses, narratives and forms that position viewers as 'foreign' to the content. The most central of these factors is the use of global media constellations—resonant figurations of form and narrative that are easily borrowed and locally refigured—which encode a preferred audience position and 'way of looking' at the objectified other.

How are audiences positioned? Certainly, audiences are active interpreters of media they consume, and media consumption is neither a homogenous nor passive practice taking place outside of particular cultural contexts. When Laura Mulvey (1981) wrote her groundbreaking analysis of Hollywood filmmaking, positing that industry conventions constructed a (male) gendered 'way of looking' through formal and narrative conventions, she was not disputing the role of reception in the construction of meanings from the text. In *Ways of seeing*, Berger's influential work on TV and gender, based on the BBC, he observed that 'according to usage and conventions which are at last being questioned but have by no means been overcome—*men act and women appear*. Men look at women. Women watch themselves being looked at' (Berger, 1972/1990, pp. 45–47). And as Laura Mulvey later argued, conventional Hollywood films not only typically focus on a male protagonist in the narrative, but also presume a male spectator through the use of formal conventions. 'As the spectator identifies with the main male protagonist', she wrote, 'he projects his look onto that of his like, his screen surrogate, so that the power of the male protagonist as he controls events coincides with the active power of the … look, both giving a satisfying sense of omnipotence' (Mulvey, 1989, p. 28).

This concept of the 'gaze' or the 'look' as constructed by dominant formal and narrative conventions, has been taken in many directions by diverse scholars, including discussions of race (Gaines, 1988), heteronormativity (Evans & Gamman, 1995; Steinman, 1992), and even the subject positioning of National Geographic photo spectators (Lutz & Collins, 1993). And while many of the Freudian psychoanalytic underpinnings of Mulvey's original conception have fallen away, the concept of 'the gaze' has remained a compelling means of conceptualizing the power of directorial conventions in visual media.

In keeping with her approach, I argue that television viewers in Indonesia are often, by default, put in a position where they are encouraged—through form and narrative—to identify with certain characters, relationships and ideologies. This identification positions them, as indeed these characters and ideologies are, as foreign to much of the culturally Indonesian subject matter that the programs deal with, be it the poor, rural characters that occasionally appear in *sinetron* largely as comic relief, or the old Javanese man exotified in a travel show like *Anak Muda*.

Let us take a single convention as an example: the following of a 'host' character with a mobile camera where the host speaks directly to the camera/viewer as though she were accompanying her on the journey: the 'following the host' constellation discussed above. We have a narrative element: we are traveling to or between places of interest; we are going somewhere, exploring with a protagonist, who is often also a source of expert knowledge. We have formal elements: the camera plays the role of the viewer, a human being who stays roughly eye-level with the host (likely using a shoulder-mounted camera). Cuts are rare, and a single point-of-view is maintained.[9] We also have a clear association between the formal and narrative elements in the simulated relationship between host and viewer that is facilitated by both the narrative and formal elements, making them greater than the sum of their parts, and resonant as a media constellation.

Without any further insight into the specific figuration of a 'following the host' manifestation, as in our *Anak Muda* case study, there is at least one important insight we can gain from the constellation alone, specifically that it is constructed around the basis of a friendship and camaraderie between host and viewer. Further, because of the host's informal expert status, the viewer is placed in a position where resistance to the boundary or agenda setting of the program's script is difficult. In other words, if one's 'expert friend' spends 10 minutes of her half-hour program discussing the *soto ayam* in a given city, one's ability to ask meta-narrative questions about the show's producers' judgment on the matter is complicated by the intimacy of the constructed relationship, and its positioning of viewer as vicarious compatriot. Add to this the representation of locals as traditional and exotic, as with the *wayang* shopkeeper, and we can begin to see how the viewer is, by default, positioned as a foreign observer of them.

In a *sinetron*, the relationship is similar, with protagonist characters almost universally of a world that is—as we have seen—foreign to its viewers both in cultural norms, styles and overwhelming wealth. Yet, of course, it is the protagonists with whom viewers are encouraged to identify, thus vicariously living out their relationship with the occasionally appearing local or 'traditional' characters, who almost invariably play marginal or comic relief roles. Even on the unconventional 2001/2002 season hit *sinetron Wah Cantiknya!*, in which the male protagonist is a 'mentally retarded' village idiot, the character is not only played for laughs consistently, but is framed by the opulently wealthy family that he has married into, including the female lead who plays his beautiful and cosmopolitan wife. The viewer's identification remains with the ambiguously wealthy family members, with narrative structures that reinforce this relationship by depicting the male protagonist as the 'fish out of water' in what would otherwise apparently be a normal situation. Thus the rural character, though he is the lead, is represented as the odd man out. And, although he is morally virtuous, his mental disability further distances him from identification with the audience and again signals a connection between rural origins and stupidity.

The use of refigured media constellations in new contexts, however, invokes a local semiotic through which the meanings of formal and narrative elements shift to serve new purposes. In the case of *Anak Muda*, we have seen how the relationship of host to local is transformed from the Western model, as producers endeavored to maintain this same distance between two Indonesians by romanticizing the local man's traditional qualities and connecting the host to cosmopolitan globalism. In other travel programs, practices such as bargain-hunting are invoked—in certain contexts—to indicate wealth and internationalism because the practice is associated, by producers, with the conventions of Western holiday travel. In practice, these are the most obvious and eye catching sorts of examples, but far from the only ones; the material kit of available media narratives may all be used in different ways and to serve different purposes than they would in foreign media. Yet my time with producers of travel shows led me to observe a broad, overlapping consensus on how many borrowed elements could become meaningful in Indonesian contexts, demonstrating specific, shared logics of derivation. Most importantly, however, this derivation of form and narrative within the cultural logic of the domestic production environment, and with the accompanying shifts in meaning and function, should give us pause before making judgments or assuming even roughly direct comparability between our own media, and outwardly similar foreign products.

Much of the norming of wealthy, culturally alien characters and lifestyles can be attributed to the foreign or international origins of producers themselves, as can be clearly seen in the country's leading production house, owned and largely operated by people of Indian descent, or in TransTV's programming department, where top executives—though Indonesian—grew up overseas. Indeed, many of their personal tastes are leagues away from the Indonesian television viewers they imagine to be their audiences—for example, one programmer confided to me his love for the British historical comedy *Blackadder*, the humor of which relies not only on a deep cultural knowledge of England and Europe, but a developed appreciation for sarcasm—a comedic style that rarely appears on Indonesian programs.

This research does not suggest that the gaze of the producer is uncritically transformed into the subject position of the spectator. However, it does raise questions about how disparities of wealth and power in developing countries like Indonesia may subtly manifest in influential mass media forms. It also points toward the importance of the shifting global mediascape—with its cultural, economic, and political logics—in domestic content production, particularly when societal élites with broad media literacy leverage ideological power over the production process. Their use of borrowed media narratives would seem to set off alarms among those who regard derivation as a failure, and the use of forms associated with Western media industries as a component of cultural homogenization. It is in the semiotic shifts that occur during the reimagining and reproduction of global constellations, however, that more localized meanings and media-cultural logics emerge, leading to globally derivative but regionally distinctive media texts.

Notes

[1] The idea of the media constellation, which I have previously discussed at greater length (Barkin, 2004), revolves around the notion that producers create new texts largely through the borrowing and reproduction of linked formal and narrative elements.

[2] 83% of advertising money is spent by corporations headquartered abroad; over 90% by corporations predominantly owned by foreign investors (ACNielsen, 2003).

[3] The producer, Tati, was an independent, working for different production companies, and occasionally for the stations themselves, in their in-house production departments. Her credits included a number of light entertainment programs, including variety and music programs.

[4] Whereas I try to avoid any reliance on, or interjection of, my own content analysis, most importantly with domestic productions, in this case I found it necessary to the discussion of Western-origin forms and narratives, to provide a larger understanding of selectivity among Indonesian producers in borrowing such structures.

[5] Although printed travel guides featuring this sort of information are now gaining in popularity, mirroring the sex-tourism industry in mainland Southeast Asia (Prideaux, Agrusa, Donlon, & Curran, 2004).

[6] 'Kampungan' or rural/'of the village' tends to carry a sharply negative connotation, and is very commonly used to dismiss anything thought to be of insufficient quality or in poor taste, not unlike the British expression 'dead common'.

[7] The only exception was an international travel series produced by a small, American-owned production house that was making the show using largely off-the-shelf footage, and was airing

it only in Balinese luxury hotels. Therefore all the programs I observed that were actually broadcast on Indonesian national television focused on domestic travel.

[8] 'Asli Jakarta'—a play on the common ethnic affiliation 'asli Betawi', which indicates the 'original' ethnic group that inhabited the Jakarta region (but see Saidi, 1997). 'Asli Jakarta' does not indicate a recognized ethnic affiliation, but rather invokes the dilution of direct affiliations that characterizes many Jakarta natives. I also got the sense that, at least in this context, it indicated that the speaker was above or at least separate from 'ethnicity' as a central factor in personal identity.

[9] This is applicable for when the host is in the shot; some programs will do multi-angle establishing or expository shots of a given destination or point of interest while the host continues a voice-over narration. When the exposition is completed, we conventionally return to the 'host and camera' configuration.

References

ACNielsen Indonesia. (1993–2003). *Television ratings data*. Unpublished. Jakarta, Indonesia: ACNielsen.

ACNielsen Indonesia. (2002). *Ratings data report, 1989–2002*. Jakarta, Indonesia: ACNielsen.

ACNielsen Indonesia. (2004, May). *ACNielsen television establishment study*. Unpublished. Jakarta, Indonesia: ACNielsen.

Abu-Lughod, L. (1997). The interpretation of culture(s) after television. *Representations, 59*, 109–134.

Abu-Lughod, L. (2002). Egyptian melodrama—Technology of the modern subject? In L. A. Faye, D. Ginsburg, & B. Larkin (Eds.), *Media worlds: Anthropology on new terrain* (pp. 115–133). Berkeley: University of California Press.

Ang, I. (1991). *Desperately seeking the audience*. London: Routledge.

Ang, I. (1996). *Living room wars: Rethinking media audiences for a postmodern world*. London: Routledge.

Appadurai, A. (1991). Global ethnoscapes: Notes and queries for a transnational anthropology. In R. G. Fox (Ed.), *Recapturing anthropology: Working in the present* (pp. 191–210). Santa Fe, NM: School of American Research Press.

Appadurai, A. (1996). *Modernity at large: Cultural dimensions of globalization*. Minneapolis, MN: University of Minnesota Press.

Barkin, G. (2004). *Producing Indonesia: The derivation and domestication of commercial television*. Doctoral dissertation, Washington University.

Berger, J. (1972/1990). *Ways of seeing: Based on the BBC television series*. New York: Penguin Books.

Bhabha, H. K. (1992). Postcolonial authority and postmodern guilt. In L. Grossberg, C. Nelson, & P. A. Treichler (Eds.), *Cultural studies*. New York: Routledge.

Evans, C., & Gamman, L. (1995). The gaze revisited, or reviewing queer viewing. In P. Burston, & C. Richardson (Eds.), *A queer romance: Lesbians, gay men and popular culture* (pp. 13–56). New York: Routledge.

Fursich, E. (2002). Packaging culture: The potential limitations of travel programs on global television. *Communication Quarterly, 50*(2), 204–223.

Gabriel, T. (1985). *Third cinema in the third world: The aesthetics of liberation*. Ann Arbor, MI: UMI Research Press.

Gaines, J. (1988). White privileging and looking relations: Race and gender in feminist film theory. *Screen, 29*(4), 12–27.

Laderman, S. (2002). Shaping memory of the past: Discourse in travel guidebooks for Vietnam. *Mass Communication & Society, 5*(1), 87–110.

Lutz, C., & Collins, J. (1993). *Reading 'National Geographic'*. Chicago: University of Chicago Press.

Mulvey, L. (1975/1988). Visual pleasure and narrative cinema. In C. Penley (Ed.), *Feminism and film theory* (pp. 57–79). New York: Routledge.

Mulvey, L. (1981). Afterthoughts on 'Visual pleasure and narrative cinema' inspired by King Vidor's Duel in the Sun (1946). In Thornham (Ed.), *Feminist film theory. A reader*. Edinburgh: Edinburgh University Press.

Mulvey, L. (1989). *Visual and other pleasures. Theories of representation and difference*. Bloomington: Indiana University Press.

Prideaux, B., Agrusa, J., Donlon, J. G., & Curran, C. (2004). Exotic or erotic—Contrasting images for defining destinations. *Asia Pacific Journal of Tourism Research*, *9*(1), 5–17.

Saidi, R. (1997). *Warisan budaya Betawi* [*Social life, customs, and history of Betawi ethnic people*]. Jakarta, Indonesia: LSIP with Pemda DKI Jakarta.

Sen, K. (1994). *Indonesian cinema: Framing the new order*. London: Zed Books.

Steinman, C. (1992). Gaze out of bounds. In S. Craig (Ed.), *Men, masculinity, and the media* (pp. 199–214). Newbury Park, CA & London: Sage.

United Nations (2003). *United Nations Development Programme/Overcoming Human Poverty*. New York: United Nations.

White, N. R., & P. B. White. (2004). Travel as transition—Identity and place. *Annals of tourism research*, *31*, 200.

Fame, Fortune, *Fantasi*: Indonesian *Idol* and the New Celebrity

Penelope Coutas

Nearly every television station in Indonesia broadcasts reality television programmes, and in the past two years there have been over 50 different reality shows produced locally but often based on or inspired by foreign formats. Replacing direct foreign imports in many cases, format adaptations of reality shows are one example of Indonesia's participation in global television and are a prominent feature of the television landscape in post-Suharto Indonesia. Although there is extensive debate over what is actually meant by reality television, the defining characteristic of the genre is that programmes are largely unscripted, the stars being real people in extraordinary circumstances who are often competing for the chance to improve their lives (Hill, 2005). Reality shows also allow viewers to 'see for themselves', which has become a key attraction, changing the relationship between viewer and screen into something more intimate and participatory than ever before.

According to ratings statistics, the periodical press, and as evidenced by fan bases, the most popular of reality programmes in Indonesia to date are singer-performer talent quests such as RCTI's *Indonesian Idol*, Indosiar's *Akademi Fantasi Indosiar* (*AFI, Indosiar's Fantasy Academy*) and TPI's *Kontes Dangdut Indonesia* (*KDI, Dangdut Contest Indonesia*). The success of these programmes has inspired spin-offs in other talent areas such as comedy, bands, acting, television presenting, and even knowledge of the Islamic faith. Of these, *Indonesian Idol* is often regarded by fans and viewers in magazines and online forums as 'the original and the best' due to its 'global glamour' and possibilities for international stardom, and it has been identified by producers and advertisers as one of the most popular reality show imports. For these reasons, *Indonesian Idol* is the focus of this study, although *AFI* and *KDI* are used as interesting points of contrast throughout.

The following will present an analysis of a new genre of contemporary celebrity in Indonesia created through reality television programmes such as *Indonesian Idol*, and examine different frameworks for approaching the fame, fortune, and *fantasi* of the show. *Indonesian Idol* is a rich source for exploring issues of celebrity production and consumption in Indonesia today, and for examining the notion of the 'active, interactive audience' within a context of globalization and increasing commercialization of cultural products and practices. Although the imaginings, meanings, and images created in and by the show may at first glance seem representative of cultural imperialism, the distinction between the 'global' and the 'local' is highly problematic, and the interactive nature of *Indonesian Idol* leads to questions of audience agency and power. *Indonesian Idol* is promoted as making the celebrity process explicit and as an example of a new, participatory, viewer–screen relationship in a glamorous, global context. But to what extent is this really the case, and what does it all mean?

Behind the Scenes: A Background to *Indonesian Idol* and the *Idola*

Indonesian Idol, based on the United Kingdom's *Pop Idol*, is a four-stage talent quest for singers and begins with televised regional auditions. In Indonesia, these take place in Ambon, Bandung, Jakarta, Manado, Medan, Makassar, Surabaya, and Yogyakarta where more than 250 from over 25,000 wannabes are chosen by RCTI and FremantleMedia executives to appear before four judges each season. A selection of those contestants then audition in Jakarta for stage two where they are whittled down to 30 by the judges. After this, the interactivity begins with viewers choosing the final 10 via SMS on their mobile phones. By this point, the singers have been carefully styled and viewers are shown clips of them selecting their outfits with the stylists and practicing with voice coaches: the 'behind the scenes' footage that helps build viewer–contestant relationships (Holmes, 2004b). Finally, there is the fourth stage, during which the final 12 contestants perform week after week as the participant with the least votes is ejected from the competition. Viewers have just over one hour between the contestants' performances in the *Spektakuler* and close of polls in the *Result Show* to vote via SMS, an essential element of the programme. No matter who is chosen and who is eliminated though, the final 12 performers have already made the transition to stardom through the mediated experience of the reality show: they have become *Idola*.

As a genre of representation, the *Idola* are a new form of celebrity: talented real people who achieve fame via reality television. This is not a phenomenon unique to Indonesia, and resembles Chris Rojek's (2001, p. 18) description of 'celetoids' who move from maximum visibility in television and magazine to complete obscurity within a matter of weeks. According to Rojek, celebrity status comes in three forms: 'ascribed' through blood relations (royal families, for example), 'achieved' in open competition (sports stars), or 'attributed' by the media (television and film personalities), and this forms a useful framework in which to position a discussion of *Indonesian Idol*'s fame process. Although there have been numerous studies conducted on celebrity and celebrification in Western academia, notably Boorstin (1963), Turner (2004), Marshall (1997), Gamson (1994), and Dyer and McDonald (1998), there has been little discourse concerning the celebrity process and industry in Indonesia.

Amrih Widodo (1991, p. 4) began a discussion of the 'celebrification of Indonesian culture' in *Bernas* magazine in the early 1990s. He tells us that the word '*selebriti*' originates from the English 'celebrity' meaning 'a person who is easily recognized by many people from many backgrounds, and often appears or becomes news in the mass media'. There is some argument over whether the term *selebriti* or *selebritas* is more *baik dan benar* (i.e. proper Indonesian; Wardhana, 2004), but it is interesting to note that neither *selebriti* nor *selebritas* appears in Echols and Shadily's (1998) popular dictionaries: a 'celebrity' is instead translated as '*seorang yang terkenal*' (someone who is well-known). Well-known for their well-knownness, perhaps? Here we find the difference between *bintang* (stars) and *selebritas* (celebrities). A *selebritas* is not necessarily a *bintang* in their field in that they are 'the best' at something. Likewise, a *bintang* may not be a *selebritas* in that a *selebritas*' life is highly visible through the media, their private lives attracting just as much interest as their professional. What is somewhat unique to Indonesia is that *selebritas* are not just film stars, athletes and television personalities, but also politicians, academics and religious leaders: the lines between *bintang* and *selebritas* are much more blurred than in Western popular culture.

What distinguishes *Indonesian Idol* and similar talent quest shows from other reality television programming in Indonesia is the emphasis on the 'democratic' voting system via SMS to 'elect' the *Idola*, and this in turn distinguishes the *Idola* from *bintang* and *selebritas*.[1] More will be said about the voting system later, but in terms of the *Idola* process, the idea of an audition process followed by a democratic vote is very important: the potential upwards social mobility afforded by these shows is promoted as being meritocratic. In 2004, Merdikaningtyas (2004, p. 3) discovered that many participants viewed the programmes and the audition processes as a form of free education, and were seriously considering a career in the entertainment industry because of *AFI* and *Indonesian Idol*. *The Jakarta Post* also commented on this change of career aspirations in a series of articles in late 2004 and concluded that:

> In the past, parents wanted their children to be doctors, engineers, lawyers or economists. With the passing of time and the advance of technology, however, more and more fathers and mothers do not mind their offspring becoming idols, actors, or vocalists. (Ryanto, 2004)

Hence there is the perception that through reality television *anyone* can be famous, if only for a short time. To return briefly to Rojek's (2001) categories then, *Idola* fame is both achieved and attributed. On one hand, to become an *Idola*, the potential star must win a competition and be the best at something—even if it is 'being the best' at gaining SMS votes, rather than singing ability—yet on the other, that fame is often 'attributed' by the media 'moment' or 'spectacle', and is dependent on media coverage. *Idola* have not replaced *bintang* or *selebritas*, but rather extended the field of possibilities. To what extent though is this celebrity status simply a construction produced 'from above'? Are the *Idola* only commodities traded by the promotions, publicity, and media industries for specific purposes?

The *Idola* Image

The *Idola* presented to the public are controlled by 'cultural intermediaries', the collective term used by Rojek (2001) to describe agents, publicists, marketing personnel, promoters, photographers, wardrobe staff and personal assistants. These people all have a role in creating the *Idola* image, as do the *Idola* themselves. They decide what clothes the *Idola* wear, how their hair is styled, how and what they sing: what 'image' of celebrity is presented during the course of the show. In developing the *Idola* image, however, producers are the most powerful cultural intermediaries. As Abercrombie (1996, p. 110) describes, the producers act as the link between the creative and commercial aspects of television. They are managers who wield substantial power, but they also act as collaborators in the creative processes. In *Indonesian Idol*'s case, the producers are from two different agencies: the national, conservative, Indonesian television station RCTI, and the international production companies FremantleMedia and its affiliate 19 Management, who created and own the *Idol* format.

The *Idol* format is the most profitable one FremantleMedia and 19 Management have ever produced and distributed. A record-breaking 1.5 billion votes have been cast worldwide for the format which is now produced in over 30 countries, including Singapore, Malaysia, Thailand and Indonesia in Asia. According to *Gatra* magazine (Guritno, Khudori, Yanuarti, Sawariyanto, & Fitriyah, 2004), the show cost RCTI tens of billions of rupiah ($1AUD = Rp. 7,000) to produce because FremantleMedia set a very high price for format rights. The format also came with a 'manual' of strict instructions that must be adhered to, and so RCTI had to buy new editing equipment and employ a specialist crew in order to meet its strict specifications. In many ways, the format itself, and not the people working within it, constitutes the most powerful cultural intermediary where *Indonesian Idol* is concerned.

In its most straightforward definition, 'a television format is a template or set of invariable elements in a programme out of which the variable elements of individual episodes are produced' (Moran, 2004, p. 5). *Who Wants to Be a Millionaire*, *Siapa Takut Jatuh Cinta?* (*Who's Afraid of Falling in Love?* from Taiwan's *Meteor Garden*), *Famili 100* (*Family Feud*) and *Indonesian Idol* are just a few examples of imported formats that have enjoyed ratings success in Indonesia. With formats, the idea for the show is imported, and not the show itself as it is with direct imports of subtitled or dubbed programmes. The framework may be foreign, but the story is local. This is important because in the last decade television ratings the world over have confirmed that, when given a choice, audiences prefer domestic and regional content to foreign programmes (Waisbord, 2004, p. 369). Formats are one effective way for television stations to cater for this fact, and so it is no coincidence that in 1999 television stations in Indonesia had more 'local' content than ever before. During the Monetary Crisis, imports became prohibitively expensive and consequently the format trade boomed, particularly with quiz show formats. In a survey of television guides from 2000 to mid-2005, local programming becomes even more pronounced from 2004

Figure 1 A Live Taping of *Indonesian Idol* at the Plaza Semanggi, Jakarta. The stage layout and studio set-up is very similar for all of the countries that import the *Idol* format. Photo by author, 24 June 2005.

onwards in the form of reality television shows based on or 'inspired by' international formats. And it is through these shows that we see the emergence of the *Idola*. In the case of *Indonesian Idol*, it is clearly the TV series that constructs, promotes, and promises the concept of the *Idola* prior to their immersion in the music industry, and it is the imported format that makes the show a commercial success. However, as Kitley (2004, p. 154) explains, 'cultural technology transfers of this type are not gifts, and are structured with the provider's profit as the prime consideration'.

As a commodity, the *Idola* are products to be marketed in their own right or to be used to market other commodities: the advertising potential of *Indonesian Idol* and the *Idola* is extremely high. According to RCTI's marketing director Daniel Hartono, advertising revenue had already exceeded 150% of expectations halfway through the 2004 season. In fact, *Indonesian Idol* had become the biggest media event for *RCTI* in three years and was close to eclipsing their broadcast of the Soccer World Cup in terms of advertising revenue (Guritno et al., 2004, p. 31). *Gatra* and *Tempo* magazines, Indonesia's answers to *TIME*, recognized this trend in 2004 and published a series of articles related to *AFI* and *Indonesian Idol* (Basral & Chudori, 2004; Guritno et al., 2004). *Gatra* made the following speculation about advertising:

> On a Friday night slot, when *Indonesian Idol* airs, *RCTI* sets the price at Rp. 18,000,000 per 30 second ad spot. Expensive? This is prime time, man! During a one hour presentation, there are six ad breaks with each break filled with roughly eight ad spots. With a total of 48 spots, in one hour *RCTI* scoops Rp. 864,000,000. Not only that, after a break of one hour, the result show phase ... takes place from 10–11pm. Here, RCTI achieves almost the same ratings, which means takings of around Rp. 1,728 billion for one episode. And that's underestimating. (Guritno et al., 2004, p. 31)

During season two, the number of ad spots rose to 17 advertisements on average per commercial break, but the advertisements were much shorter individually than those of season one. In a newsletter published in August 2004, the media research group ACNielsen gave a report highlighting *Indonesian Idol*'s ratings success compared to its two main rivals, *AFI 3* and *KDI*. They found that during the commercial breaks of *AFI 3*, most viewers tuned into *Indonesian Idol*, and vice versa during the *Indonesian Idol* breaks. The introduction of *KDI* influenced viewer choice further, but more people watched the final moments of *Indonesian Idol* than the other two programmes (Nielsen Media Research, 2004, p. 6). Although it is questionable how Nielsen Media Research obtained their data, the fact that they published this account in a widely read and distributed industry newsletter is significant. In 2004, *Indonesian Idol* was the star of the ratings game (at least according to ACNielsen, *Gatra*, and *Tempo*), and its advertising was presented as reaching the highest number of (target) consumers.

The Marketing Value of *Idola*

Ratings success for television programmes invariably means the stars become recognizable and have greater commodity value as signs. The *Idola* were, and are, also contracted by various companies to market their products. This is especially true for Delon, the runner-up of *Indonesian Idol 1*, whose *cakep* (handsome–trendy) looks made him a success with both fans and advertisers. The judges also became 'faces' for headache tablet *Paramex* and *Mustika Ratu* face-whitening lotions. Add this to the product placement throughout the show of sponsors' products and services and it is easy to see why some authors argue that reality television is 'advertainment': the merging of advertising and entertainment programming that creates a new type of consumer culture (Berger, 2003; Deery, 2004).

For June Deery (2004), reality television's primary purpose is to sell. Sponsors become part of the show, central to the narrative, and not just a 'frame' before the extended commercial break. In *Indonesian Idol*, the *Idola* are often seen using *Fren* network cellular phones while eating *Indomie* instant noodles and wearing certain designer clothes. From Deery's perspective, every part of the programme is a commodity, especially the *Idola* themselves, and so the real story of the programme is to 'sell, sell, sell'. According to Aditya Indrawanto, an account executive for Matari Advertising who manages *Fren* and *Indomie*'s advertising, product placement on *Indonesian Idol* has been a highly successful strategy for his clients. Product sales had increased since they began advertising on *Indonesian Idol*, especially amongst 'tier one' of the population. Indrawanto felt that the 'exclusive' and 'foreign' feel of *Indonesian Idol* attracted these tier one consumers to the show, and that this in turn had boosted his clients' sales considerably with the target group (Indrawanto, personal communication, 2005). In many respects then, the real 'consumers' of *Indonesian Idol* are the advertisers themselves, whilst 'the audience' (as produced through ratings) constitute the product.

Highly surprising in terms of marketing and merchandizing though is that the merchandizing for *Indonesian Idol* is nowhere near as extensive as that of *American*, *Australian* or *Canadian Idol* and other adaptations. The product list for these countries is extensive: single song releases, albums, posters, DVDs, books, t-shirts, temporary tattoos, key chains, karaoke machines, and a CD-ROM computer game are just a few of the items available to fans. In Jakarta, for instance, although there were *Indonesian Idol* albums available for sale (both official and pirated) mid-2005, and t-shirts were produced on the black market for season one, there was very limited merchandizing available at the live Friday concerts for season two, and none available at regular shops and stalls other than the album releases. Compare this to *AFI* with its huge availability of merchandizing and even an online store. In 2004, sellers found it extremely profitable to sell *AFI* trading cards, writing paper, wallets, pins and key chains outside primary schools. These trading cards had specific street value and if an *Akademia* were to win the most SMS votes that week, their card's value would increase. *Indonesian Idol*, however, has no such merchandizing available. At the concerts, balloon-sellers told me that the producers were very strict about copyright and they were not allowed to copy the *Indonesian Idol* logo. Their balloons and signs were only permitted stencilled outlines of the names of contestants, which they made to order. Selling balloons for Rp. 10,000 each (roughly $1.40AUD), one seller told me they would make enough profit to be worthwhile, but he felt they could earn a lot more if they were allowed to use the *Idol* logo.

The Sign of the *Idola* Image

The *Idol* logo is a readily identifiable sign in global television and by virtue of this has great power both in terms of marketing value and in creation of meaning. It is doubtful that the balloon-sellers would have been able to purchase the rights to use the *Idol* sign and still make a profit at Rp. 10,000 per balloon. From a semiotic perspective, we find many signs throughout *Indonesian Idol*, not only the logo, all of which are part of the global *Idol* brand. The blue colour scheme, the theme music, the slogans, the stage, the editing style and camera angles, the 'nasty judge' and the 'nice judge', the lights and character montages: all of the elements that create the format are in themselves a sign system. This sign system is consistent across different countries' adaptations of the show, which makes the format clearly identifiable across cultures and locales.

In approaching the *Idola* from this same perspective, we gain a greater understanding of their commodity value as images or signs. Like the logo, the *Idola* image has value in both the market and cultural economies. As Marshall (1997, p. 57) relates:

> Like the sign, the celebrity *represents* something other than itself. The material reality of the celebrity sign—that is, the actual person who is at the core of the representation—disappears into a cultural formation of meaning. Celebrity signs represent personalities—more specifically, personalities that are given heightened cultural significance within the social world.

This perspective can be applied to analyses of the *Idola*. It is not the *individual* contestant on *Indonesian Idol* who has immediate exchange value, but rather the concept or idea of the *Idola* and what the *Idola* represent. After all, anyone can be an *Idola* and, in the end, it does not matter who wins from the production companies' profit-making perspective. They do not even have to be good-looking, as proven by the very overweight Mike who won the season two competition, or follow the mainstream faith, as with Joy, the Christian gospel-singer winner of season one. The record companies are guaranteed a platinum, if not multi-platinum album, and the television producers have a well-rating show no matter who wins: the *Idola* are interchangeable.

The *Idola* as a Global Brand

When asked which show they thought was 'better' out of a choice *of Indonesian Idol I, Indonesian Idol II, AFI* and *KDI*, more than 80% of 150 survey respondents from universities and high schools in Jakarta, Yogyakarta, and Bali chose one of the *Idol* shows. Their reasons? It was like *American Idol*, it was better 'quality', and it did not just mimic a foreign show: it was the same as the foreign original.[2] No doubt the ability to compare *Indonesian Idol* and *American Idol*'s sign systems aided these conclusions, as *American Idol* was broadcast by RCTI immediately prior to *Indonesian Idol*'s seasons. Although *AFI* or *KDI* may have been respondents' favourite shows, *Indonesian Idol* was consistently regarded as better *quality*. Since *AFI* was in production long before *Indonesian Idol*, and in fact TransTV's *Popstars* preceded them both, why is it that *Indonesian Idol* was still regarded as 'the original' and 'the best' by respondents?

Many survey and interview participants were adamant that the global nature of *Indonesian Idol* distinguished it from the other reality television shows. The fact that the *Idola* would have the opportunity to 'go international' and participate in *World Idol* and *Asian Idol* was a recurring theme in survey responses about the quality of the show. Throughout both seasons, the global nature of the programme was constantly reiterated by the show's hosts, with many references to *World Idol* and past *Idola*'s success overseas. There were also crossovers between *Indonesian Idol* and other countries' versions—Clay Aiken, an American Idol, visited tsunami-stricken Aceh; Guy Sebastian, an Australian Idol, sang with some of Indonesia's season one *Idola*; and the winner of *The Philippines Idol*, Christian Bautista, performed at the *Indonesian Idol 2* Grand Final. That the *Indonesian Idol* series one winner, Joy, quit her contract because of the producers' reluctance for her to 'go international' straight away caused an uproar of public opinion in the tabloid press and online bulletin boards. Many viewers wrote in these forums that they felt cheated that Joy did not have the opportunity to compete on *World Idol* in 2004, and that RCTI and FremantleMedia's management team were to blame. In season two, the producers were much more careful not to make promises about a second *World Idol*, but instead focused on *Asian Idol* to be held in late 2005. In any case, the global nature (in terms of both distribution and participation) of *Indonesian Idol* and possibilities for the *Idola*'s success at the international level remained central to the show's promise of stardom.

Imperialistic *Idola*?

The idea of *Idola* as a global brand leads to questions of cultural and media imperialism. Indeed, the cultural imperialism thesis is initially a very attractive one for explaining the messages of *Indonesian Idol*. Herbert Schiller (1976) proposed the use of the term 'cultural imperialism' to describe and explain the way in which large multinational corporations, including the media, of developed countries dominate developing countries. For proponents of the cultural imperialism thesis, global television is colonizing television. In Indonesia, the idea of cultural influence from the West (mainly America) through the medium of television is not new, and has been a long-standing concern (Kitley, 2000, p. 103). In *Indonesian Idol*'s case, the contents of the show are recognizably 'Western'. Not only did the format originate from the West, first in the UK and then American, but the *Idola* image is also of the West. That is, the portrayed 'globality' of what they represent is identifiably Western, and of Western culture.

Culture is understood here as widely distributed systems of symbols through which people make sense of the world in order to orient themselves, construct identities, and communicate with others (Peterson, 2003). Media producers necessarily draw on these same symbolic systems in order for the representations they create to be meaningful for viewers. With *Indonesian Idol* there is a tendency for global culture to be equated with Western culture, and it is a one-way flow. For example, the *Idola* sing songs and engage in a performance style from the Western 'pop' and 'rock' traditions rather than from more uniquely 'Indonesian' forms such as *dangdut* (see Weintraub, this volume) or 'traditional' Indonesian music. This in turn makes *Indonesian Idol* familiar to foreign audiences and gives it a foreign, or at least international, feel for local audiences. The 'Indonesian' of *Indonesian Idol* is tokenistic: the *Idola* occasionally wear *pakaian adat* (traditional dress) on State visits, they have their own theme song, and there are many 'background information' scenes about the *Idolas'* home towns and support networks. However, these characteristics are part of the prescribed format, and are consistently adapted across every country's version of the show, and this is not something unique to the Indonesian case.

The Indonesian press has critiqued *Indonesian Idol* for valuing one style of cultural performance and celebrity over another, that is, the Western pop tradition over more recognizably 'Indonesian' types. *The Jakarta Post*, in particular, has been highly critical of *Indonesian Idol* and reality television's 'effect' on Indonesian mass culture. Although *The Jakarta Post* journalists were initially enthusiastic about the show and reported on its potential for invigorating the music industry, by the end of 2004, articles were much more negative in tone and expressed the opinion that many of the reality television shows in production were having a detrimental effect on Indonesian culture. In September, a feature article stated,

> Entertainment or reality shows should not necessarily be banned. But anything which threatens to retard the country's intellectual development should be shelved. Otherwise our society will get dumber as our neighbours get smarter. ('Dumb and dumber', 2004)

The label most often used in the mass media to express the idea that a society is experiencing a marked cultural decline is 'dumbing down'.[3] Like many other labels employed to describe developments in the socio-cultural sphere, it is decidedly imprecise. Since the early 1990s, however, 'it has been applied to a wide range of artefacts and phenomena and has been frequently mobilized to indicate the user's disapproval that cultural life is being increasingly subject to commodifying and globalizing forces' (Kilborn, 2003, p. 26). It is interesting that the journalist quoted above was wary of 'our neighbours get[ting] dumber' when all of Indonesia's closest neighbours (Malaysia, Singapore, Australia) have themselves imported the *Idol* format, and exchange *Idola* with Indonesia both in promotional exercises and via the music charts. Perhaps the journalist was following a more general trend of commentators overseas to classify reality television formats such as *Idol* as 'mindless entertainment' (Hill, 2005). For these analysts, reality television has low 'cultural capital', to use sociologist Pierre Bourdieu's term, and therefore will have little value in the cultural marketplace. Then again, the reason the journalists were fearful is because, in Indonesia, these television shows have *high* cultural capital: they are representative of a global network of exchange and of participation in a global community—they have a 'global glamour' that is promoted and presented by producers and advertisers as being highly desirable.

The *Idology* of *Indonesian Idol*

John Thompson (1984, p. 4) proposes that 'to study ideology, is to study the ways in which meaning (or signification) serves to sustain relations of domination'. Returning to the framework of cultural imperialism, then the West is dominating Indonesia with this import. In other words, the ideology of *Indonesian Idol* is an *Idol*ogy of global glamour and of capitalist consumption values, represented through the *Idola* image. The 'meaning' of *Indonesian Idol* and the *Idola* serve to sustain the relations of the West being the 'ideal' and participation in a global network of celebrity as being the ultimate accomplishment in the entertainment world. To 'go international', particularly to Western countries, is promoted as the ultimate desire. The ideology of Indonesian Idol represents something other than just a new pathway of *selebritas* status, and demonstrates the adaptation or change of local cultures. From this perspective, *Indonesian Idol* is a direct example of cultural imperialism, and represents a one-way flow of values and ideas. The 'Indonesian' aspects of *Indonesian Idol* are a facade for a foreign cultural import.

However, the cultural imperialism thesis is not without its critics, and there are dangers in only considering this perspective. Some authors argue that the thesis overstates the power of the global as a straightforward extension of Western (particularly American) power, and understates local responses to the global. The situation is much more complicated because societies are not necessarily 'passive recipients' of whatever product, company or media is thrust upon them. Critics and revisionists of the thesis assert that the economic component of media imperialism may be expressed in statistics, but the cultural component is more difficult to measure (see Sreberny-Mohammadi, 2002). Furthermore, they argue, audiences are active producers of meaning and produce a diversity of readings.

Therefore, the cultural imperialism thesis is a limited one for analysing the popularity and influence of *Indonesian Idol*. Although the format is highly prescriptive and it is not necessarily *Anda yang memilih* ('It's you who choose', the catchcry of season one), a centre–periphery model that pits 'the West' against 'the Rest' is inadequate to explain the global flows of cultural technologies associated with *Indonesian Idol* and the *Idola*. Many writers on the subject argue that globalization does not necessarily mean cultural homogenization, and local audiences apply their own cultural competencies when making meaning from and adapting foreign texts. Arjun Appadurai (1996), for instance, suggests that global trends intersect with local practices to create disjunctive local patterns of production and consumption. His key point is that simplistic centre–periphery models are inadequate to explain the impact of globalizing cultural flows, which he summarizes as ethnoscapes, mediascapes, technoscapes, finanscapes, and ideoscapes that are ever-changing. From this perspective, *Indonesian Idol* is one landmark in a complex system of global messages, and one that is influenced by (and influences) a wide range of cultural texts, values, understandings and ideologies. Although the format may have originated in the West, the local aspects of it remain critically important, and they are not tokenistic. It is those aspects that are appealing to viewers and fans, who interpret them in a variety of ways for their own purposes.

'Feeling Glocal' with *Indonesian Idol*

Annabelle Sreberny-Mohammadi (2002, p. 353) has identified the need for an alternative approach to globalization and media products, 'one that recognizes and does justice to the dynamic tension between the global and the local, and the shifting terrains they encompass'. She calls this outlook 'the global in the local, the local in the global', a very similar approach to Koichi Iwabuchi's (2004) description of 'feeling glocal', and lends another, alternative, framework for approaching the production and consumption of *Indonesian Idol* and its *Idola*.

In business jargon, 'glocal' means taking a global view of the market, but making adjustments for local considerations. Rather than implying the disappearance of the local through standardization the term highlights the linking of locales and the flow of ideas and technologies between them. As Iwabuchi (2004, p. 34) describes,

> ... the format business has given audiences a pleasure in sharing the common frameworks *and* the irreducibly different appearances that manifest in local consumption. Put differently, what is being promoted is not simply 'global localization' that aims to adopt the common to the difference but also 'local globalization' that makes audiences feel 'glocal', that is, a sense of participation in a global society through the reciprocated enjoyable recognition of local (in most cases, synonymous to 'national') specificities articulated through the shared formats.

Clearly, *Indonesian Idol* is an example of 'feeling glocal' because it is a local adaptation of a global product. If the winner of *Indonesian Idol* were to participate in *World Idol*, then there would also be an outward transfer, and the *Idola*'s songs have the potential to climb the music charts outside of Indonesia. Rather than diminishing or 'corrupting' local cultures then, foreign format imports such as *Indonesian Idol* offer another forum for the expression of local culture and celebrity within the paradigm of global television: it has not replaced any 'Indonesian' form, but has extended the field of possibilities. Before *Indonesian Idol* and other reality television programmes were broadcast in Indonesia, Western imports predominated in those timeslots. These were mainly direct, subtitled or dubbed, imports of films and dramas or sitcoms. They have now been replaced by local productions, albeit foreign formats, or as *Gatra* headlined, '*Program Impor, Idola Lokal*' ('Imported programme, local *Idola*', 15 May 2004). Furthermore, fans of the show are not restricted to Indonesia alone, and are part of a global community. Participation in the *Idol* experience, therefore, is a transnational experience: it is participation in a global community from a local level. It is glocal.

On the other hand, notions of global and local cultures, and of global and local celebrities, are relational. The local is often defined in opposition to the global and, in the cultural imperialism thesis, in opposition to the West. But, as we can see with *Indonesian Idol*, the distinction between the local and the global has become complicated and problematic. There are definite local aspects of the show, but these can also be interpreted as tokenistic and prescriptive—a mere 'ethnic tinge', reinforcing the hegemonic cultural order in which global, Western-based forms dominate. Are they *really* local, or are they global? Moran (1998) argues that formats are not the catalysts for cultural sameness or the loss of cultural diversity; adaptations provide opportunities for reimagining nations in various ways. Hence, *Indonesian Idol* provides opportunities for reimagining celebrity, culture, and the nation in various ways, and this is not uniform. It is also not uniquely 'Indonesian'. This is a phenomenon shared by many locales, and not all of them 'Western'. From one perspective, *Indonesian Idol* is an example of cultural imperialism; from another, it is an example of cultural hybridity and pluralism. Others still see the reinvigoration of Indonesian pop music through *Indonesian Idol*, or it can be approached as an example of 'feeling glocal'. What analysis of these different perspectives reveals is an example of how producers are imagining Indonesia's position in the global cultural flow when they develop strategies of glocalization. At the very least, Indonesia is an active participant in this global flow, and the *Idola* are representative of a global phenomenon of a new type of television celebrity, and a new television audience.

Idolizing 'the Audience'

While the media construct the public visibility of the star (proposes them for election), it is the audience (as electors) who determine their degree of success (Holmes, 2004b, p. 167). Rather than being commodities created by foreign production industries to sell other commodities, or part of the West's quest for global cultural homogeneity, the *Idola* signify a new trend in celebrity production and consumption: direct democratic election via an interactive process. The audience (and not the producers, the text, or the institutions) have the power in determining the outcome of this cultural product. Indeed, this is explicitly advertised by *Indonesian Idol* with the catchcry of '*Anda yang memilih, Anda yang menentukan!*' (It's your choice, your decision!) at the beginning and end of every show. But is this just a *fantasi*? Just how interactive, and active, is this 'interactive audience', and how much power do they *really* have? To begin to answer these questions, let us first determine who 'the audience' actually are.

Philip Kitley (2000, p. 110) in his book on Indonesian television describes RCTI's audience as being perceived as: 'a collection of well-off consumers who enjoy a materialistic lifestyle increasingly influenced by international styles and values'. It is clear from commentators' accounts, advertising on RCTI, and articles in the periodical press that *Indonesian Idol* is aimed at those middle to upper class 'well-off consumers', especially teenagers, who live in the major cities of Jakarta, Surabaya and Bandung. The *dangdut* talent quests such as *KDI* and *KonDang-in* are aimed at a different population, as is *AFI* with its emphasis on regional districts rather than Jakarta that appeals to all ages. However, to make generalizations about *Indonesian Idol*'s audience as *only* those well-off teenage consumers is problematic and relies on many assumptions that treat individuals as a generalized group, or a 'mass' rather than 'active viewers' of varied tastes.

'Active viewing' is the notion of viewers *engaging* with television programmes, often through what Stuart Hall (1980) has described as the 'encoding/decoding' process. From this perspective, although texts are 'structured in dominance' leading to a 'preferred meaning', the audience may not necessarily understand the texts in the same way the creators intended, they may totally ignore the message in favour of just enjoying the image, or even read television broadcasts proactively in the political sense. They may also appear to take no notice at all of what they might be watching (Nilan, 2001 p. 86). Anthropologists go one step further to argue that interpretation of television messages is a social *act*, a performance by particular persons in particular situations and seek to understand the ways in which people encounter media texts in everyday life and how this shapes their reception of, and active engagement with, them (Peterson, 2003). It is beyond the scope of this article to discuss the many theories of the audience here. But, in favouring an anthropological perspective, it is important to understand the viewing context of *Indonesian Idol*'s audience, and to identify that the assumption that 'the audience' are those 'ABG' (*Anak Baru Gede*—literally 'children newly big' or the 'yuppie' equivalent) and '*anak gaul*' ('trendy youth') is largely correct within this context.

The Viewing and Voting Context

The *ABG* viewers of *Indonesian Idol*, particularly in Jakarta, encounter this multimedia text in a saturated fashion in their everyday lives due to the impact of new media convergence. Understanding the sheer volume of advertising and media texts related to the show that are being accessed (actively and passively) is highly significant when approaching the audience of *Indonesian Idol*. In June of 2005 when the show was mid-season, numerous Jakarta and Surabaya shopping malls had signs urging fans to '*nonton bareng*' (watch together) in their cafes, mobile phone providers pushed downloading of *Indonesian Idol* ringtones, no teen magazine was without *Idol* gossip, and *Indonesian Idol* CDs had prime positions in music stores. These are just a few examples of what was available in addition to the relentless advertising on RCTI, most notably the *Indonesian Idol* logo in the top right hand corner of the screen during every other show. The text itself was also multi-platform with its website and mobile phone components offering what Will Brooker (2001) calls 'media overflow': an immersive, participatory experience which extends the 'text' of the show beyond the time and space in which it is broadcast. It was impossible to be unaware of *Indonesian Idol*, especially if you were of that 'target audience' who shopped at the malls, owned a mobile phone, and read magazines and websites. Hence, the audience of *Indonesian Idol* had a very immersive environment in which to access this media text, and it is easy to assume this would have an impact on how they would respond to, and interact with, the show.

In my surveys of this 'target audience', however, I discovered that only a small proportion of respondents actively sought out supplementary non-television media sources related to *Indonesian Idol*. Almost all had watched the show on television, chatted about *Indonesian Idol* with friends both face-to-face and via the phone, seen billboards and advertising, and heard songs on the radio. But less than 20% of respondents had actively gone to *warnets* (internet cafes) to seek out more information, buy tabloids specifically for *Indonesian Idol* coverage, or buy official merchandise. This was also reflected in SMS voting. As described earlier, an essential element of the show is the 'democratic' SMS and premium call voting. Contrary to popular advertising and newspaper reports of a 'frenzy of voting' and 'revenue

Figure 2 *Indonesian Idol 2* Contestants on a Promotional Tour at a Jakarta Shopping Mall. Photo by author, 2 July 2005.

raising', many viewers of *Indonesian Idol* surveyed do not actually participate in the voting process. Only nine respondents from a sample of 150 had actually ever voted, and only four with any regularity. From those 150 students, almost all had seen the show, and over 80% were regular viewers. Many survey respondents wrote that they did not like the SMS and telephone polling system—they thought Indonesian people would vote with their hearts, and not their heads. In other words, they would choose 'the best' singer based on their background and looks rather than voice quality. Many also described their dislike of the reality show's timeslot. Considering it is at 10 pm on a Friday school-night, many felt cheated that they would not be able to watch the results, even if they did vote.

In contrast, from my surveys of 60 audience members at the live concerts for *Indonesian Idol*, a very different picture emerges. Seventy-three percent of respondents reported that they regularly voted via SMS or telephone for their favourite *Idola*, some spending up to Rp. 500,000 (roughly AUD$70) a week on votes and most averaging Rp. 10,000 to Rp. 50,000 (AUD$1.40–$7). Their reasons for voting were just as the other respondents feared: many of the studio audience based their decisions on primordial ties with contestants, and then on 'voice quality' and 'friendliness'.

In the act of voting, we can see a definite distinction between *viewers* and *fans* of the show. Bielby, Harrington, and Bielby (1999) explain that the difference between a television viewer and a television fan is an important one. To 'view' television is to engage in a relatively private behaviour, but to be a 'fan' is to participate in a range of activities that extend beyond the private act of viewing and reflects an enhanced emotional involvement with a television narrative. Long time fans, moreover, develop a 'metatext', consisting of a detailed knowledge of the history, themes, and running jokes associated with a television show and create a great deal of discourse about their own media consumption (Peterson, 2003, p. 151). Therefore, being a fan of *Indonesian Idol* involves more than an affective orientation towards a 'distant other' and requires active engagement with media texts.

There was a great deal of difference in survey answers between declared fans at the show and randomly selected participants from the universities and schools, which verifies the descriptions of fandom above. The fans interacted and accessed many more supplementary materials than the viewers, and actively sought out possibilities for that interaction. They bought CDs, participated in mailing lists, bought magazines and tabloids, visited *warnets*, attended meet-n-greets, made t-shirts and placards, and actively sought out like-minded fans. It is clear though that the definitive fan action is participation in the voting process. This activity reflects both enhanced emotional and economic involvement with the *Idola* narrative and defines the 'ethnographic moment' in which viewers become fans. Overall, the fans were, and are, far more interactive in their activity than the viewers.

Strong *Indonesian Idol* fans then are not 'passive viewers' subject to 'media effects', but engage in television viewing, and take action based on that engagement. Rather than the more traditional celebrity–fan relationship, whereby the fan 'is seen as being brought into (enthralled) existence by the modern celebrity system, via the mass media' (Jenson, 1992, p. 9), the process is inverted. The *Idola* are understood to be a result of the fans—as a response to the ratings system, and to their voting. The fans' support is paramount for the creation of the *Idola*. This is why *Indonesian Idol* fans are almost always called '*pendukung*' rather than '*penggemar*' or even 'fan'. *Penggemar* is the Indonesian equivalent of the English term 'fan', from the Latin, '*fanaticus*', originally meaning 'of the temple', becoming a reference for certain excessive forms of religious belief and 'excessive enthusiasm' (Jenkins, 1992, p. 12). '*Pendukung*', however, translates as 'supporter'. Before the emergence of the *Idola*, '*pendukung*' predominantly described the supporters of sporting stars and groups, and of politicians and political parties. Their agency is seen as central to those peoples' success. And so it is with the *Idola*. Just as the talent–quest reality shows have created a new genre of celebrity, there is now also a new genre of fan: the *pendukung*, the creators and supporters of *Idola*, and not a response to their creation. This is not to say that the *pendukung* have replaced the *penggemar*: rather the *penggemar* in this case more closely resemble the 'viewer' as described above, whereas the *pendukung* are the more active, interactive 'fan' without whom the *Idola* would not exist.

Issues of Interactivity

As Tincknell and Raghuram (2004, p. 201) explain in their analysis of *Big Brother*, 'the idea of "interactive" media texts makes the idea of the active audience newly interesting because it suggests that such audiences may go beyond simply responding to a text—they may also help to change it'. Although the concept of 'interactivity' is ambiguous, it has gained increasing currency in relation to television, 'articulating a rhetoric that insists pressingly upon a 'new' participatory relationship between viewer and screen' (Holmes, 2004a, p. 213). This has prompted critics to re-examine the concept of the active audience that have been so central to debates in media and cultural studies. Some approach this in a positive light (the audience are participators and not just passive viewers), and others in a more negative one (it is a gimmick employed to grab viewer attention, nothing more). However, we must remember that this is not a new phenomenon, even in Indonesia. Magazines have had confessional advice columns for years, the 1980s saw talent quests premiering on *TVRI*, and AnTeve's *Gol Gol Gol* in 1995 featured a machine that could fire footballs at high speed controlled by call-in viewers using their push-button telephone handset (Barkin, 2001). Moreover, Indonesian audiences have a long history of direct interaction with other forms of media, especially performance texts such as *wayang kulit* (shadow puppet) plays and dance presentations, from entering into dialogue with characters to performing themselves. It can be argued that Indonesian audiences have *always* interacted with media texts, and the idea that reality television in its participatory style is something entirely new is misleading.

What *is* new with *Indonesian Idol* is that the interactivity between audience and text is explicit, and the *idea* of agency is central to its success. This begs the question:

Figure 3 Glenn's (*Indonesian Idol* Season Two) Supporters at the Plaza Semanggi, Jakarta. They were unable to buy placards that used the official *Idol* logo. Photo by author, 24 June 2005.

to what extent is it a *fantasi* of agency that is constructed 'from above'? Holmes (2004a) suggests that understanding the extent to which such programmes offer a space for audience intervention in, and negotiation with, contemporary cultural production requires a resistant reading that dismantles the rhetorical structures of the text itself. She argues that it is a naïve view of the audience to think they have control, because their intervention in reality programmes is carefully orchestrated, managed, and curtailed (Holmes, 2004b, p. 165). After all, they are told when to vote, why to vote, and how to vote. This is certainly evident in *Indonesian Idol*'s voting system where the *pendukung* have to take it on face value that the voting system is not corrupt: at no time is voting data revealed. Additionally, the voting process itself is highly regulated in being restricted to the various confines of the programme's format. It is not until the second phase of the show that viewers and fans have an opportunity for direct interaction, and even then it is restricted to a specific time frame and socio-economic group. During the entire process then, the *pendukung* are at best choosers rather than actors, and their activity is always prescribed. But this does not mean the audience are powerless. As choosers, they determine the *degree* of success of the *Idola* who have been constructed by the media, and in this way their interactivity via the voting system has a direct effect on the show's outcome. In

Indonesian Idol, moreover, the audience is presented with (carefully constructed) opportunities for resistance, and the election of what some consider non-mainstream choices, such as Mike and Joy, might be considered as such. In this way, the *Indonesian Idol* text becomes a site of negotiation, or struggle, between encoded messages and the decoding process: between the messages 'from above', and 'from below', and between the imaginings of the media professionals, and that of the audience.

Conclusion

The imagining presented in *Indonesian Idol* is one that is certainly popular, but whether as an aspirational imagining of the middle and upper classes or a source of bemusement is open for debate. There is a 'global glamour' about the programme and its stars: there is no doubt that the *Idola* image as an interchangeable commodity sign has great value in both the economic and culture industries. If we view the *Idola* 'from above' as commodities traded by the promotions, publicity, and media industries, then the show's primary role is to extend and reinforce the role of capital, and of Western ideology. The *Idola* identity being created by and in *Indonesian Idol* represents certain perceptions of the social world, and certain cultural under-standings. The fact that this form of celebrity and celebrity process originates from the West, and is created by an identifiably 'Western' format, is highly significant.

However, from another perspective, *Indonesian Idol* is an example of cultural hybridity and pluralism in 'feeling glocal'. The social function of the *Idola* image is one of bridging the local and the global, and demonstrates Indonesia's participation in global television flows. The possibilities afforded by the programme for the *Idola* to 'go international' are considered vitally important by fans and *Idola* alike, and the fact that these wannabe celebrities depend upon a democratic election is central to the format. The audience, especially the *pendukung*, could possibly be described as 'active choosers'. The audience imagines it determines the degree of their *Idola*'s success, and their support is paramount for not only their favourite contestant's potential fame and fortune, but also the continued viability of the show. *Indonesian Idol* makes the celebrity process explicit, and audience agency always features within this process, even if it is prescribed.

I argue that *Indonesian Idol* is not an example of the local or the global, the East or the West, the producer or consumer, the audience or celebrity; but something else again. We need to resist the binary logic which seeks to comprehend cultural products via mutually exclusive terms and recognize the emergence of a shared space. *Indonesian Idol* is representative of an understanding of celebrity that circulates globally, and the fact that so many audiences (especially teenagers) relate to the franchise so well all over the world is indicative of this. This understanding goes beyond 'glocalization', and represents new expectations of the viewer–screen relationship and of global cultural products. It may be a certain type of world culture, heavily commercialized, and quite exclusive, but it is glamorous and attractive because of this, at least for the Indonesian audience surveyed. Perhaps the global fame of *Indonesian Idol* is only a promise and not a fact, but it certainly captures the imagination, and the SMS votes.

Notes

[1] The Indonesian press made many correlations between the voting systems on reality television programmes and Indonesian democracy during the lead-up to the 2004 Presidential elections. For an analysis of this and other links between performers and politicians in Indonesia, see Lindsay (2005).

[2] This survey questionnaire was undertaken over three weeks in June of 2005 with 90 first-year students from Universitas Indonesia, Jakarta; Universitas Gajah Mada, Yogyakarta; and Universitas Udayana, Denpasar, and 60 final-year high school students at SMUN8, Jakarta and SMA3, Yogyakarta. Their responses were contrasted with 60 surveys distributed to similarly-aged audience members at two 'live' *Indonesian Idol* tapings. Respondents were asked a series of open- and closed-answer questions concerning viewing habits, opinions on reality television in general, and talent quest programmes and *Indonesian Idol* in particular. Although the sample space was small, their responses gave anecdotal evidence that proved an interesting point of contrast to advertisers', fanzine, and producers' accounts.

[3] Interestingly, in Indonesian-language newspapers and periodicals, the phrase 'dumbing down' is often borrowed directly from English. Colloquially, in relation to television, the concept is also expressed through the saying '*kebanyakan nonton televisi bikin otak mandul*' ('too much television makes one's brain barren').

References

Abercrombie, N. (1996). *Television and society*. Cambridge: Polity Press.

Appadurai, A. (1996). *Modernity at large: Cultural dimensions of globalization*. Minneapolis: University of Minnesota Press.

Barkin, G. (2001). Oldest trick in the book: Interactivity and market interests in Indonesian television. *Media/Culture Reviews*. Retrieved March 18, 2005, from http://www.media-culture.org.au/reviews/features/interactive/gbarkin.html

Basral, A. N., & Chudori, L. S. (2004, August 29). Indonesian Idol dan AFI: Song of Joy [Indonesian Idol and AFI: Song of Joy]. *Tempo*, 71–76.

Berger, W. (2003, March). That's advertainment! *Business 2.0 Magazine*, 90–95.

Bielby, D. D., Harrington, C. L., & Bielby, W. T. (1999). Whose stories are they? Fans' engagement with soap opera narratives in three sites of fan activity. *Journal of Broadcasting and Electronic Media*, 41(1), 35–52.

Boorstin, D. (1963). *The image*. London: Penguin.

Brooker, W. (2001). Living on Dawson's Creek: Teen viewers, cultural convergence, and television overfly. *International Journal of Cultural Studies*, 4(4), 456–472.

Deery, J. (2004). Reality TV as advertainment. *Popular Communication*, 2(1), 1–20.

Dumb and dumber. (2004, September). *The Jakarta Post*. Retrieved March 3, 2005, from http://www.thejakartapost.com/Archives/

Dyer, R., & McDonald, P. (1998). *Stars*. London: BFI.

Echols, J. M., & Shadily, H. (1998). *Kamus Inggris Indonesia: An English-Indonesian Dictionary*. Jakarta: Penerbit PT Gramedia Pustaka Utama.

Gamson, J. (1994). *Claims to fame: Celebrity in contemporary America*. Berkeley: University of California Press.

Guritno, G. A., Khudori, Yanuarti, Sawariyanto, A., & Fitriyah, N. (2004, May 15). Duit mengalir sampai jauh [The money flows far]. *Gatra*, 30–31.

Hall, S. (1980). Coding and decoding in the television discourse. In S. Hall (Ed.), *Culture, media, language: Working papers in cultural studies, 1972–79*. London: Hutchinson.

Hill, A. (2005). *Reality TV: Audiences and popular factual television*. London: Routledge.

Holmes, S. (2004a). 'But this time you choose!' Approaching the 'interactive' audience in reality TV. *International Journal of Cultural Studies, 7*(2), 213–231.

Holmes, S. (2004b). 'Reality goes pop!' Reality TV, popular music, and narratives of stardom in Pop Idol. *Television & New Media, 5*(2), 147–172.

Iwabuchi, K. (2004). Feeling glocal: Japan in the global television format business. In A. Moran, & M. Keane (Eds.), *Television across Asia: Television industries, programme formats and globalization* (pp. 21–35). London: RoutledgeCurzon.

Jenkins, H. (1992). *Textual poachers: Television fans and participatory culture*. New York: Routledge.

Jenson, J. (1992). Fandom as pathology: The consequences of characterization. In *The adoring audience: Fan culture and popular media* (pp. 9–29). London: Routledge.

Kilborn, R. (2003). *Staging the real: Factual TV programming in the age of big brother*. Manchester: Manchester University Press.

Kitley, P. (2000). *Television, nation, and culture in Indonesia*. Athens: Ohio University Centre for International Studies.

Kitley, P. (2004). Closing the creativity gap—Renting intellectual capital in the name of local content: Indonesia in the global television format business. In A. Moran, & M. Keane (Eds.), *Television across Asia: Television industries, programme formats and globalization* (pp. 138–156). London: RoutledgeCurzon.

Lindsay, J. (2005). *Performing in the 2004 Indonesian elections. ARI Working Paper Series 2005*. Retrieved September 12, 2005, from The National University of Singapore, Asia Research Institute Website, http://www.ari.nus.edu.sg/docs/wps/wps05_045.pdf

Marshall, P. D. (1997). *Celebrity and power: Fame in contemporary culture*. Minneapolis: University of Minnesota Press.

Merdikaningtyas, Y. A. (2004). Mimpi-mimpi menuju bintang [Dreams of becoming a star]. *KUNCI, 14*, 3–7.

Moran, A. (1998). *Copycat television: Globalisation, program formats and cultural identity*. Luton: University of Luton Press.

Moran, A. (2004). Television formats in the world/the world of television formats. In A. Moran, & M. Keane (Eds.), *Television across Asia: Television industries, programme formats and globalization* (pp. 1–8). London: RoutledgeCurzon.

Nielsen Media Research. (2004, September). Battle of two: Indonesian Idol and AFI 3. *Nielsen News Indonesia*, 6.

Nilan, P. (2001). Gendered dreams: Women watching sinetron (soap operas) on Indonesian TV. *Indonesia and the Malay World, 29*(84), 85–98.

Peterson, M. A. (2003). *Anthropology and mass communication: Media and myth in the new millennium*. New York: Berghahn Books.

Rojek, C. (2001). *Celebrity*. London: Reaktion Books.

Ryanto, T. (2004, April 23). Local TV stations slave to 'idolatry'. *The Jakarta Post*. Retrieved March 3, 2005, from: http://www.thejakartapost.com/Archives

Schiller, H. I. (1976). *Communication and cultural domination*. White Plains, NY: M. E. Sharpe.

Sreberny-Mohammadi, A. (2002). The global and the local in international communications. In K. Askew, & R. Wilk (Eds.), *The anthropology of media: A reader* (pp. 337–356). Malden, MA: Blackwell.

Thompson, J. B. (1984). *Studies in the theory of ideology*. Cambridge: Polity Press.

Tincknell, E., & Raghuram, P. (2004). Big brother: Reconfiguring the 'active' audience of cultural studies? In S. Holmes, & D. Jermyn (Eds.), *Understanding reality television* (pp. 252–289). London: Routledge.

Turner, G. (2004). *Understanding celebrity*. London: Sage.

Waisbord, S. (2004). McTV: Understanding the global popularity of television formats. *Television & New Media*, 5(4), 359–383.

Wardhana, V. (2004). *Stamboel Selebritas* [*The celebrity stage*]. Jakarta: Kepustakaan Populer Gramedia.

Widodo, A. (1991). Kebudayaan selebriti dan selebritisasi kebudayaan [Celebrity culture and the celebrification of culture]. *Bernas*, 4, 11.

Entertaining Illusions: How Indonesian Élites Imagine Reality TV Affects the Masses

Mark Hobart

If broadcast television is the private life of the nation (Ellis, 1992, p. 5), what does a study of contemporary Indonesian TV tell us about people's lives? And what do Indonesians make of television and how it impinges on their lives? However potentially important, the topic is enormous and inchoate, as we are dealing with some 250 million people spread across an archipelago and differentiated by language, religion, class, gender, age and interests. Since the 1970s television has played a key role in how the political élite has imagined and interpellated the population. With the emergence of commercial channels in the early 1990s, most broadcasting, whether terrestrial or satellite, has comprised 'entertainment' in a broad sense. More specifically, since 2002, certain surprising kinds of reality TV have become highly popular and have attracted extensive concern and commentary. So I wish here to consider how they imagine and address their audiences, why they have generated such controversy and who is perturbed by such programmes.

Approaching the themes of entertainment—and so reality TV as entertainment—raises problems:

> Everyone knows what entertainment is. It is obvious. Except that as soon as we begin to talk about it we get into a muddle ... Entertainment is difficult to define *because* everyone knows what it is, because it is a common-sense idea. (Dyer, 1992, p. 1)

So what constitutes good sense behind the common sense? And what counts as entertainment, for whom and according to whom? As televised entertainment presupposes audiences to be entertained, what do—and can—we know about what such a variety of viewers are up to, how, when and under what circumstances? What kind of research might appropriately address these questions? By this point it becomes clear that the whole issue is caught up in a host of presuppositions, which include *a priori* notions of how humans engage with media—here television. Such accounts largely ignore empirical issues, such as the historical and cultural contexts of viewing, discussion and use, not least because such contexts are extremely diverse and often unknowable. Moreover, these accounts assume analysts can get inside individual viewers' minds to know what they are actually thinking or feeling—a perduring European dream of surveillance and control (Foucault, 1977). The detailed study of what audiences make of what they watch, be it entertainment or otherwise, remains an intractable problem.

One of the reasons we have difficulty in thinking critically about what is entertaining, and for whom, lies in a collusion between media industries, media studies scholars, and sections of the political and economic élite. It involves a closure, which assumes the content, meaning and mode of reception of broadcasting are sufficiently determined somewhere between the process of production and the surveys, articulations and interpretations of media commentators and scholars as effectively to anticipate, and so obviate, the need for critical empirical inquiry, whether of production, distribution, reception or use. Such an account suits the political élite, as it gives them the impression they are both listened to and know how they are being received by their imagined audiences. No wonder then that, however clumsy and incoherent entertainment might be as a folk category, its use perseveres. It enables the neat, if fanciful, predetermination of how broadcasting is supposed to work and programming is to be received. The alternative would spell uncertainty and the recognition of a potential threat to political, social and industrial élites insofar as television has emerged as a key means of articulating, regulating and surveying populations in most contemporary societies (Poster, 1990, p. 49). But how does all this bear on something as seemingly innocent as reality TV in Indonesia?

Background

The former President Suharto's resignation in 1998 and the titular end of the New Order with the scaling down of state apparatuses of surveillance and censorship of the media preceded a period of remarkable enthusiasm and exploration across much of the mass media. Besides a rejuvenated film industry, print and broadcast media have flourished. Particularly striking is the emergence of local broadcasting, with regional, local and community television stations and innumerable radio stations flourishing.[1] With one state television broadcaster and 10 national terrestrial channels, over 50 local stations and a plethora of other satellite and cable channels for the wealthier, Indonesians have, it would seem, a rich viewing life. There are differences and inequalities though. The range of free-to-air television channels is not equally available throughout the country, with the rural poor in the remoter provinces having the least access, sometimes limited to the public broadcasting channel TVRI. State television is still recovering from being partly dismantled as a national network and is trying to redefine its public role from the days when it was widely considered a propaganda arm of the Suharto régime. While a slew of weekly magazines celebrate, preview, review and offer some background on the more popular programmes on the commercial stations, the opinion and correspondence columns of the main broadsheet newspapers periodically lament and lambast the excessive commercialism of television and its influence upon ordinary people. With the relaxation of censorship, there seems a new energy and drive among commercial broadcasters, with intermittent attempts to innovate, or at least to pilfer and adapt (or 'dub') foreign formats, if only to try to keep market share and attract advertisers.

With so much entertainment television, one is spoilt for choice. Several considerations focused my interest upon two genres of reality TV. They were at once popular and the topic of much discussion in the media themselves. They are popular, in the sense of being about ordinary people and aimed at a popular or mass market.[2] They have also engendered extensive public debate and concern about the dangers of television as entertainment, to the point that government empowered the Indonesian Broadcasting Commission (KPI) to regulate such broadcasts.[3] This debate was also significant in that a whole range of public figures took it upon themselves to pronounce on what was good—but mostly bad—for the masses, so defining themselves not only as arbiters of taste, but as the authoritative articulators of the social and political order. In this sense such figures position themselves as self-proclaimed members of the élite. I take it that such an élite is not necessarily a fixed entity, but variously constitute themselves through different sets of social relationships, of which the mass media are one.

Interestingly the programmes that attracted all this public attention are *prima facie* not about entertainment at all. The first genre, emerging out of serious television news, is coverage of crime stories and social violence. The second would seem to have more to do with that most serious of topics—religion—notably in its idiosyncratic Indonesian inflection of interest in the supernatural (the paranormal, mysticism).

Evidently a neat division between serious and entertainment broadcasting does not necessarily work well here.

These crime (*kriminal*) and occult (*mistik*) programmes flourished between 2002 and mid-2005, by which time the scheduling time, especially of the latter, had declined.[4] The former deals with ordinary people—notably as perpetrators, victims and witnesses of violent crime. The latter offers glimpses into private, or semi-public but unseen, worlds in which ordinary people—again as victims, witnesses, believers or sometimes as protagonists—are caught by television cameras. Both genres are also interesting because the public discussion they provoked was largely in the print media. That is to say, they involve inter-media commentary and are informative about the complicated relationship of television to print. These two genres also are interesting because they are part of a broader global trend towards 'reality TV', however understood (Andrejevic, 2004; Brenton & Cohen, 2003; Holmes & Jermyn, 2004; Kilborn, 2003). Without the cost of stars, scriptwriters, expensive sets or camera equipment, and where the 'realistic' effect of the hand-held DV camera and cheap lighting are an asset rather than a defect and with mass audiences, the television companies are laughing all the way to the bank. So the stage was set for argument about the value and dangers of such programming, in which the audience was predestined to be the shuttlecock.

The Rise of Crime on Television

So far I have been unable to pinpoint exactly when *kriminal* emerged as a separate genre from general news broadcasts on mainstream channels.[5] For example, Indosiar, the market leader in audience share of crime coverage, aired its hour flagship crime programme, *Patroli*, at midday, followed by *Jejak Kasus* (*Investigating Cases*). In the same slot, SCTV countered with *BUSER* (an acronym from hunt, *Buru*, and arrest, *Sergap*). SCTV also hosted an in-depth late evening criminal investigation programme, *Derap Hukum* (*Footsteps of the Law*). On some channels, like SCTV, straight news broadcasts also included crime coverage. RCTI, in keeping with their up-market image, mostly restricted themselves to a twice weekly daytime show, *SERGAP*, while the other channels struggled to develop distinct offerings. Two stations departed from the trend in differing degree. TransTV had developed a late night high profile investigative programme, *Kupas Tuntas* (*In-Depth Analysis*), which tackled serious issues like corruption. And state television with its more Reithian brief avoided such programmes, which contributed to its declining, indeed minuscule, market share nationally.

By 2004 every commercial channel had on average one to two hours a day of violent crime coverage. For the more celebrated crimes, several channels would vie for coverage, each offering rival reconstructions, analyses and interviews with witnesses. Rumour had it that, the more sensational the crime, the more the station would have to pay the police to be first on the scene. While the standard format was reportage accompanied by interviews with witnesses, the victim (if alive), family and local police, Indosiar also ran a one-hour programme reporting the police point of view on crime, based on lengthy studio interviews. The naming and exposure of victims and corpses make actual individuals identifiable—in life and in death. Through suffering, members of the masses, however briefly, attain identifiability, as persons or, rather, as victims and evil-doers.

With so many competing channels, differentiating product by style and branding became important. At one end television station Lativi had come up with a formula that neatly summarized its programme, *BRUTAL*, an acronym from *BeRita UTama kriminAL* (*Important Criminal News*), which had something of an ironic cult following among the university students I knew. At the other TransTV, although a newcomer, under Ishadi SK, the former head of TVRI, was aiming for poll position among the serious channels. Their riposte was an extraordinary late night programme *Menanti Ajal* (*Awaiting the Hour of Death*). This consisted of a series of detailed investigations by a smart young Jakartan woman journalist, Andromeda, into the background of well-known murders. This included detailed exploration of the scene of the crime where possible, lengthy interviews with the families of the perpetrators and with the prisoners who had been condemned to death. One programme included her musing on life as seen from inside the condemned man's cell and joining the inmates for meals. Unlike the other programmes, the journalist reported her feelings and reflected on the nature of such strange assignments before returning in each episode to Jakarta and a suitably luxurious setting where she would play a white grand piano to the closing credits—a variation on the (presumably unintended) theme of crime and class.

Crime as Real

How was crime imagined and portrayed on television in these shows? With their historical links to news, it is hardly surprising that most real-life crime programmes were presented in the documentary mode[6] used by news broadcasting. Shots of the scene of the crime or accident were obligatory, ideally with close-ups of the corpses as discovered (otherwise sometimes reconstructions inter cut with forensic photographs) or in the morgue. For non-fatal incidents, clips of victims were, where possible, accompanied by live interviews. Multiple witness accounts lent further colour and immediacy. Scoops however comprised footage of the police going into action; or the suspect being interrogated; or arrestees dragging themselves across police stations floors having been shot (as is conventional) in the leg or thigh. Failing that, footage showed the accused in clothing carefully marked *tersangka* (suspect) confessing or reconstructing the crime. Hand-held cameras recorded the situation: shots of the victims injured or dead, in hospital or the morgue, but ideally at the scene and as 'realistic' or grotesque as possible.

The structure of these programmes obeyed the hierarchy of clawback (Fiske & Hartley, 1978, p. 87), where the reporter structures events and the statements of the victims, witnesses, suspects and police into the conventions of the genre. In turn, the studio anchor frames the whole process through questions directed to the reporter; and by explaining to the audience what it is they are watching and how to understand it. Reality TV helps determine what counts as reality. As with much Indonesian television, the presenters were almost always attractive upper middle class young women, mostly fashionably dressed, sometimes accoutred to suggest a certain solemnity to the proceedings. Although traffic accidents, public brawls and, occasionally, terrorist acts were featured, the meat of most programming was family or domestic violence—the very family life that media commentators are concerned to protect from exposure to violence on television. Granted how much emphasis the New Order and television advertisements put on fantasizing the family as the harmonious natural unit of social life, the exhibition of the family—or at least lower class families—as the site of strife stands in ironic contrast.

For programmes claiming to access the realities of violent crime, mostly we heard little from those intimately involved.[7] When they were allowed to speak, suspects almost always articulated their motives in terms of brute passion—usually greed or anger. Close relatives alternated between disbelief, surprise and resignation. Witnesses were shocked and horrified. In taut phrases, police summarized events and demonstrated themselves (*ex post facto* at least) to be in charge. Except for short clips, as when docile suspects painstakingly confessed,[8] the programmes relied on voiceover. Middle class reporters' voices framed and explained the violent crimes mostly perpetrated by a quite different sector of society—the working class and underclass. Where the victims were middle class, the coverage was generally more extensive and the tone one of perplexity. Middle class crime—nepotism, fraud, corruption—rarely featured in *kriminal*. Crime is implicitly identified with specific classes, whose carefully edited accounts fit highly structured stereotypes. When people were allowed to talk about their lives in another emerging genre of reality TV, that is, investigative reporting on the urban underclass,[9] they often came across as remarkably coherent, moving and reflective about their predicaments. So Indonesian crime programming emulated much reality TV in scrupulously avoiding reality, while claiming the opposite.

Instead of attempting to impose ideas of objectivity and representation on *kriminal*, it may be more helpful to think of them, anthropologically, as ritual, which I take to consist in pervasive modes of pre-articulation, designed to anticipate the awkward recognition of incoherencies and antagonisms in society. *Kriminal* arguably is about structuring and containing fear. Put this way, *kriminal* are rites of class, involving crucially the exposure to public gaze, and the spectacle of humiliation, of the lower classes. That these last comprise the bulk of the audience raises intriguing questions. So does what *kriminal* does within the context of family life, on which it provides so scathing a commentary. On this account television viewing is not just about entertainment but modes of interpellation which ritualize the implication of persons within society in different ways.

Supernatural Reality Shows

How Indonesians are positioned within reality TV becomes more complicated when we move to the genre which briefly eclipsed crime in popularity. Indonesia has a long history of film and television production about the supernatural, often linked to horror. After media liberalization, commercial stations started to broadcast low budget stories about the supernatural for evening viewing. By 2002, almost every channel had slots devoted to *mistik*. The market leader was RCTI's KISMIS *Kisah Misteri* (*Mystery Stories*), comprising re-enactments of occult encounters told by ordinary people interviewed by a striking, beautifully dressed and internationally educated presenter, Caroline Zachrie. Later RCTI, like other channels, added interactive phone in. However, the chronotopes—ideas of space, time, narrative, character, causation and agency (Bakhtin, 1981)—remained much the same. They just became more demotic, as 'ordinary people' could recount in the studio, or phone in with, personal experiences.

Although they are hardly the first to cash in on popular ideas about the supernatural, Indonesian television channels have turned the supernatural into a distinctive mode of reality show. TransTV lead the way with its mid-evening programme, *Dunia Lain* (*The Other World*). Programmes are of several kinds. There are 'true life' stories of mystical occurrences re-enacted by professional actors. The themes are usually gruesome events that seem to defy scientific explanation, but bear the authority of invited eye witnesses. Others are pseudo-documentary, such as TV7's *Expedisi Alam Ghaib* (*Expedition into the Invisible World*) when a team of 'experts' seek to establish the background of places with a history of mystical disturbance, commonly involving attempts to photograph ghosts and similar beings.

Much more spectacular and enduring has been Lativi's *Pemburu Hantu* (*Ghost Hunters*), in which a team of idiosyncratically adorned, headscarf wearing, Muslim *ustadz* (religious teachers) each week visited a haunted house, where the perturbed owners reported on uncanny disturbances, after which, amid much drama and somersaulting, the *ustadz* chased down the ghosts, before finally capturing them in empty soft drink bottles. Meanwhile another meticulously blindfolded *ustadz* painted each ghost on a large white canvas.[10] To add 'independent corroboration', celebrity guests were placed in an empty room and were later asked to compare what they saw with the paintings. The middle class owners invariably expressed great relief and appreciation for the exorcism. By 2005 Pemburu Hantu had moved to regular two-hour live broadcasts with an additional backdrop of rows of 'ordinary people', many of whom spirits would enter and whom the *ustadz* had to bring back to normality.

Dunia Lain explored quite different possibilities by combining the supernatural with hardship challenges. Members of the public volunteered to survive for a night in locations painstakingly described by local experts as exceptionally mystically dangerous. Clips of the ordeal, recorded on DV cameras on night-light function, were edited against the soundtrack of a loudly clicking clock. Afterwards the subject reported his or her experiences, which almost always coincided with the hallmark signs of that spot. After senior religious figures complained, TransTV introduced a short closing disquisition by a religious figure (usually Muslim, sometimes Hindu or Christian) explaining that such phenomena were known to the religion in question, but were harmless provided proper religious etiquette were observed.

Other programmes are more tongue-in-cheek. TransTV ran a late night show, aptly named *Paranoid*, when people would target a suggestible or timid friend, who was then set up in a deserted spot, where mysterious sounds and sights were engineered, while the victim's terror was scrupulously recorded. The end comprised the victim and friends resolving feelings by laughing over what happened. Not all victims found it amusing. TPI's late evening show, *Ihhhh Seremmm* (*Oooh Hair-Raisinggg*), did a take-off of the others using candid cameras to record members of the public being tricked by spoof occult moments. Other episodes were direct commentary on their rivals, as when a senior ghost-buster incanted manifest mumbo-jumbo before his naïve acolytes. When one remarked on the ghastly smell ghosts made, the ghost-buster replied, 'No, I just farted!' Reality supernatural TV is not without critical commentary within the medium itself.

The popularity of these and other genres of reality TV may be interpreted as a reaction against the rigidity and formulaic nature of most broadcasting under the New Order. An example is the endless series of implausible soap operas about a tiny handful of metropolitan mega-rich, which once dominated prime time and the ratings. As Alfadin, a TV director and scriptwriter, remarked:

> nowadays on television the range is broader. So the theme of mystery can be drawn out in any direction. So it isn't monotonous. It's just natural if people nowadays are sick and tired of programmes which just portray wealth (The theme of mystery is a reflection of depression. (5 March 2003, *Kompas*)

Speaking as a foreigner who has been watching Indonesian television since the late 1980s, I found the supernatural programmes fun to watch for a time. The settings were different; there was an appearance of unpredictability.[11] They mostly involved the sorts of people you might meet in the street, presented as human by contrast to the conventional tableaux of self-important public figures and government officials, who still appear with monotonous regularity in news bulletins and current affairs chat shows. Anecdotally, most people with whom I discussed *mistik* stressed similar themes. Part of the appeal of reality TV seems to be that it was the antithesis of the patently engineered charade of television under the New Order. However, audiences have histories and tastes change: a point not lost on contemporary broadcasters. As already noted, by 2005 the viewing figures for *mistik* had reportedly started to fall and air time was down.

How are we to understanding the popularity, however transitory, of such programmes? The search for one unifying explanation may be misplaced, because with *mistik* we are dealing not with a single genre, but diverse programmes cobbled together from disparate sources, united only in expatiating on what lies outside conventional worlds. Indeed '*mistik*' can refer to anything from spooky, to paranormal, occult, supernatural or mystical as the irrational. However, what the different forms of *mistik* across the mass media share is the antipathy they arouse among certain sections of Indonesian society.

Such programmes are also informative about how—or indeed whether (see Barkin in this collection)—Indonesian television producers thought about their audiences. With adherents of all the world's major religions in the archipelago, what can you assume about your audiences' preconceptions, predilections and vulnerabilities? To the extent that programmes depend upon the dramatic, at times riotous, display of spirit worlds frowned upon by most formalized religion, what are the implications of such coverage? Even if the producers are playing to widespread popular beliefs, there are complex implications both for official religious authority and for the canons of rationality upon which models of modernity and development at least notionally rely. That *mistik* manages to offend all the major religious and secular authorities suggests the reasons for its popularity are not necessarily simple.

Comparing *Kriminal* and *Mistik*

How do *mistik* and *kriminal* programmes differ? Both portray largely non-élite worlds. While *kriminal* highlights the underclass, *mistik* often deals with stories and encounters of more established social groups. Both address themes of the complexities of human (and non-human) motivation, conflict, transgression, victimhood, the establishment of agency and responsibility and usually the re-establishment of social order. Whereas the *raison d'être* of *kriminal* is violence and excessive emotion, these elements vie with others in *mistik*. This is interesting in itself, because studying local healers often reveals a murky world of pure instrumentality, extreme violence and intense human feeling and motivation. Far from exaggerating, programmes about *mistik* may actually sanitize what goes on.

What *mistik* programmes have in common is the recognition—indeed often celebration—of a non-manifest world that works according to presuppositions that differ from and defy those of the normal social and political world. So *mistik* offers a potential challenge to public power and inequities. It also provides a rich seam of commentary as to what constitutes 'normal' in the first place. *Mistik* threatens the social and political order, by maintaining that there is another order which is not only beyond the control, or even comprehension, of the élite, constituted as modern and rational. *Mistik* works by different rules and taps sources of power that purport to be superior and insubordinate to the mundane world. Mysticism has long been a popular theme in Indonesia among all social classes, perhaps most famously in Java. As it surfaces in *mistik*, mysticism is commoditized and demotic, and it flaunts its difference from both formal religion and rational modernity at once. Insofar as it challenges rational modernity, it negates the basis on which the political and economic élite claims publicly to found its legitimacy.

Is *mistik* then a liberatory or emancipatory genre, a means of disputing accepted understandings about power and position? The programmes I have watched do not so much challenge current ideas of power and propriety as reassert equally fixed, but more 'traditional' ones and, as such, comprise a conservative response to uncertainty. The diegetic structure of *mistik* remains largely conventional. Recognized experts are called in to deal with disorder, rather as do the police in *kriminal*. The ghosts and other perpetrators are captured, exposed, sometimes interrogated. The hierarchy of society is not threatened. This may explain a striking feature of the seemingly unscripted remarks made by contestants in *Dunia Lain* and other shows. Considering the potential openness of the situations they encounter, the protagonists' *ex post facto* accounts of their experiences are remarkably standardized. Either the other world is structured along lines at least as rigid as this, or else the language or constitution of experience itself is strongly pre-articulated.

Finally, how are the participants and the audience positioned in *mistik*? The terms of participating in occult programmes are quite different from crime. (Generally you do not volunteer to be mugged, raped or murdered.) However, the constraints on what those involved can say are somewhat similar. Reporters, presenters, experts and studio anchors are on hand to articulate the participants' experience for the viewers. This is not entirely to foreclose imaginative invention, which may seep through and so confirm apparent authenticity and unscriptedness.

How viewers position themselves in relation to *mistik* is, I think, more open than *kriminal*, where the risk of the audience empathizing with the suspects is usually minimized. This openness touches on a feature of some reality TV, namely, the invitation to the audience to engage with the terms of reference themselves—a possibility rigorously eschewed in *kriminal*. The challenge is explicit in the title of ANTeve's *Percaya Nggak Percaya* (*Believe or Don't Believe*). A favourite topic of discussion among viewers I have watched and worked with is whether they believed in the supernatural in general and whether any particular episode was real or faked. Another popular theme was technological. What tricks did the TV companies use to help the non-manifest manifest itself? Viewers' scepticism became a way of attracting them to watch and question what they see. If that is indeed part of Indonesian reality TV, treating viewers as sufficiently mature as to make up their own minds implies a multifaceted relationship between broadcasters and public. That, certainly, is how a senior producer chose to present his channel's position:

> Making up their minds about television programmes, including supernatural, should be left up to viewers' wisdom. As a mirror of reality of ordinary people, every television genre is impermanent because it is always developing and changing.

> I think that the belief that television programmes cause deterioration in people's way of thinking is taking things too far. After all the public are able to make up their own minds according to whatever values they profess' (said the CEO of PT Televisi Transformasi Ishadi Sutopo Kartosaputro, 27 August 2003, *Kompas*)

However, audiences become increasingly skilled at viewing. And viewers subsequently turned off *mistik*.

How Élites Imagine the Masses

Appreciating that viewers change with and through television broadcasting, which is transitory and volatile, might seem the end of the matter. Is it not just harmless diversion? Some people who claimed to speak for part or all of Indonesian society, however, thought otherwise. The leading broadsheets regularly reported conferences and publications, and published opinions by leading citizens, which routinely condemned crime and supernatural programmes, and lumped them together with *pornografi* and *pornoaksi*.[12] Interestingly there seemed relatively little difference in orientation between the Muslim *Republika* and the Catholic-run *Kompas*.[13] Both could be direct. For example, a *Republika* headline read: 'Come on, let's sort out rubbish broadcasting' (26 August 2004). *Republika* would also invoke explicitly religious criteria, as when it warned that *mistik* programmes were *syirik*—i.e. to be avoided on religious grounds.[14] For *Kompas*, the broadsheet favoured by much of the mainstream political and intellectual élite, the 'influence' of television was a theme to which columnists and opinion-writers returned regularly.

The starting assumption of much broadsheet coverage was neatly summed up in the headline 'Behaviour is influenced by frequency of television-viewing' reporting on the award of a doctoral thesis in Gadjah Mada University which took it as axiomatic that television did in fact influence behaviour. What was at issue was the relative impact of education, consumer lifestyle, family environment and religious adherence in minimizing television's baleful influence.

> Redatin [the author] suggested that ordinary people should become intellectual and discriminating television viewers ... Moreover, before watching, family members should also be required to study or to finish other duties first. If possible, place the television set somewhere where it does not attract attention, advised Redatin. (Central Java section, 26 July 2003, *Kompas*)[15]

Several presuppositions need comment. Implicitly 'ordinary people' are lazy and shirk chores, are easily distracted and must be discouraged from indulgence. Entertainment is *ipso facto* bad. The argument enshrines a grim view of human nature—or rather of 'ordinary people'. What is their weakness? Is it that they are not intellectual? Is it they are liable to be influenced by what they see? Is it that they are not middle class? The term used to distinguish such people is *masyarakat*, society, which I translate as 'ordinary people' or 'the populace' according to the context. In every article I have read to date, *masyarakat* were people 'out there', on whom reason had a weak grip and who were prone to influence, emotion and recidivism. They were defined by lack. *Masyarakat* has taken over from a previous term, *rakyat*, the public at large, the masses, which is no longer so acceptable, with its connotations of *rakyat yang masih bodoh*, the masses who are still ignorant. Remarkably, *masyarakat* never seemed to include the writer, who stands apart as the knowing subject who, by mysterious means, understands those who are incapable of knowing themselves. It is in this self-defining sense that I use the term élite here, not to impute any coherence or essence to them.

A subsequent intervention by the deputy head of the national committee on human rights directly addressed the impact of *kriminal*.

> The common people of course need criminal news. However presentations full of violence are exceedingly negative for the development of society. First, opinion will be formed that violence is legitimate for suspects and criminals ... Second, incessant news about criminality with a high level of violence will create an atmosphere of fear among ordinary people ... The situation is deeply alarming because it can give rise to a paranoid populace. (16 April 2003, *Kompas*)

Here the base proclivities of *masyarakat* were taken as given and set unequivocally against the rational demands of the modern state. Moreover, the general populace were so primitive they had not even basic powers of discrimination. They lacked any sense of proportion, critical capacity or ability to recognize representation and genre. Television threatens to pathologize the masses. Even on cursory inspection, the argument fails to hold up. As these common people are the ones most likely to meet such violence in their daily lives—because *their* violence is being portrayed—who exactly is gripped by fear and paranoia? It is the only subjects about whom the writer can realistically know in intimate detail—the middle classes.

An interesting debate was sparked by *Kompas* publishing an opinion poll of unspecified Indonesians on 25 August 2003, under the not-entirely-neutral banner 'Swallowing whole dreams and violence from television presentations' (Menenggak Mimpi dan Kekerasan dari Sajian Televisi). The piece involved a struggle between the writer's opinions and the statistics cited which contradicted the argument.

> By presenting the programmes it makes, it is judged that television can herd the public into being in the position of receiving all the illusory sensations in the world of *sinétron* [television series], violence and eroticism that have become an inseparable part of life.

What was behind this was the sheer popularity of television. Citing an earlier ACNielsen study, the article stated that over 80% of people aged over 15 chose television as their source of information, and also noted that the majority (79%) of respondents 'admitted' they often watched broadcasts of criminal news. Considering the rapid change from sanitized, indeed lobotomized, broadcasting under Suharto, to a more open media environment, most people seemed to be coping pretty well.

> Music and talk shows which reek of eroticism and films are deliberately presented in order to seduce viewers for the sake of nothing other than profit. As a result, violence and eroticism are nowadays regarded as commonplace because people are used to watching them on television. This was expressed by half the respondents who could accept the violence and eroticism on television as not excessive ... As a result, apart from viewers never being educated with programmes of quality, even the information that was presented tended to bewilder ordinary people. Such confusion about the information they got from television of this kind was experienced by half (52%) of respondents.

Ignoring the possibility that the responses suggested a fairly open-minded, tolerant and reflective sample, struggling perhaps to cope with rapid change, *Kompas's* columnist had to perform mental gymnastics to reach the contrary conclusion.

The next day *Kompas* fired a second barrel under the banner 'Supernatural Programmes on Television Stunt Logic' (Tayangan Mistik di Televisi Tumpulkan Logika, 16 August 2003). Citing Suharlan, the Director of General Intermediate Education and 'an expert on television', Effendi Gazali, from the University of Indonesia, began:

> Television stations have forsaken their mission as part of development of the nation's mind with ever more incessant supernatural presentations on television screens. In chasing revenue targets, the whole world of television executives have so easily allowed themselves to become subject to advertisers in broadcasting things that stunt logic and are the exact opposite of reason ... 'In the long run children will think that, without learning or even working hard, life can improve. This is because supernatural broadcasting tends to present solutions to problems by non-logical means' said Effendi ... 'Our level of thinking will regress by several centuries. Faced with pupils who have been stuffed with mystical ideas, teachers will have difficulty explaining in a logical way how natural phenomena or chemical reactions happen' [Suharlan] explained.

It is not the masses, but the experts, who are confused. The philosophical notions of logic and reason stand in a complex relationship to natural science and all these to modernity, which is a historical process. Likewise, the experts reiterate familiar confusions between practical and pure reason, and between reason and absolute presuppositions (Collingwood, 1940).

More interesting is Effendi's observation that children will think that life can improve without learning or even working hard. Granted the virtually insuperable obstacles to the poor in Indonesia improving their lot, however hard they study or work, the supernatural arguably offers at least as rational and realistic a chance of success. However, there is indeed a category of Indonesian children for whom life is far more likely to be good, or even improve, without study or hard work. And that is the children of the rich. Effendi's comments are counterfactual and obfuscatory.

A reply to the *Kompas* articles was not long in coming. A fortnight later Ishadi issued a sharp retort.[16] As former head of state television, then CEO of TransTV, he was hardly a disinterested party. However, he was evidently better informed than the experts not only about the television industry and changing world trends, but media theory. Ishadi questioned assumptions that audiences are passive and easily influenced by arguing they could equally be imagined as discriminating. What was more, trends in television are volatile. So, jeremiads against television are usually exaggerated or misplaced.

Among the points Ishadi made was the experts' confusion over what conclusions may be drawn from quantitative as against qualitative analyses. While the former may be useful for determining certain kinds of conscious engagement and so setting advertising rates, by the 1970s qualitative research was already recognized as far superior for understanding audience engagement with television. The conjunction between advertising and low programme quality was facile and failed to understand the responses to audiences by television as a culture industry. As the most important sector for advertisers was the highly educated A & B socio-economic status group, stations had to attract them with high quality broadcasting. Finally he challenged the simplistic mechanical connections underlying accounts of influence and argued that, in Saudi Arabia with draconian censorship, incidence of rape was very high, whereas in liberal Indonesia it was low. He concluded by dismissing the direr claims about television's effects as concocted and simplistic. That discussion in *Kompas* subsequently returned largely to parading prejudice as incontrovertible scientific fact is itself a commentary on the rationality of Indonesia's intellectual élite as it constitutes itself in the print media.

Imagining Audiences

The repeated articulation of modernity with an idealized 19th century vision of natural science and reason is hardly unique to Indonesia, but is common sense, not good sense. What interests me here is the bearing all this has on how people, whatever their other differences, distinguish themselves as members of a certain class or group as qualified to enunciate on behalf of the nation or society as a whole and, in so doing, distinguish themselves from those they write about.

On the accounts above, this élite stands apart from the masses, who are characterized by lack. They are objectivized by collective terms like *masyarakat* or *rakyat*, as anything from a category to be manipulated, objects to be fashioned or primitive beings to be trained into socially constructive behaviour. The imagery is mechanistic. It is about behaviour, not the actions of subjects who reflect on, and try to change, the conditions of their lives through various practices, including television-watching. There is little, if any, recognition of ordinary people as working, suffering, thinking, feeling and engaging with the world through the mass media as part of often complex lives with histories. Nor did the experts attempt to reflect on incoherencies in their received ideas of television, the mass media or even entertainment itself.

Why do most commentators insist on denying their participation in the general public?[17] *Kriminal* and *mistik* become means for distancing this élite from what they enunciate on. The masses are *Autre* (others as objects) not *Autrui* (others as subjects) through whose recognition you attain your own sense of subjecthood. So what drives this determination *a priori* to objectivize most Indonesians and to ignore the obvious complexities of how people engage with television in their lives? *Kriminal* and *mistik* form two frightening faces of the masses. The danger is that, in watching criminality, the masses will see themselves and their predicaments reflected and grow to fit the mask. Moreover, dwelling on criminality permits the camera lens to turn—as the bolder investigative journalists occasionally try—to the far graver crimes committed by the rich and powerful. In flirting with the supernatural, the masses are articulating the world according to a quite distinct apparatus of causation, of justice and injustice, of power, which acts as a sardonic commentary on the doings of their masters. Significantly this other world stands in what Baudrillard (1990) described as a 'seductive' relationship to the bourgeois world.[18] Class antagonism and hetero-geneous forms of power and knowledge are themes that have been endlessly reworked in distinctive ways in Indonesia. If the disjunctures of power, class and mutual understanding in contemporary Indonesian society run so deep though, how easy would it be to change them to create the more democratic society which reformists seek?

Are we, however, merely describing the more general global working of capitalism, refracted in class divisions or globalized television formats? After all, reality shows, be they real-life crime, ordeals or candid camera, did not originate in Indonesia. While political-economic and mass communications approaches to Indonesian television provide an initial frame of reference, they leave much unexplained. Notably they omit any reference to how Indonesians understand, judge and engage with their own media. The relationship of religion, power and class in Indonesia with its myriad of patrimonial régimes has long puzzled scholars, infuriated outsiders and intrigued Indonesians themselves—which last is what much television is about, while remaining 'incomprehensible for anyone outside its scope' (Ellis, 1992, p. 5). Television is not just an industry but comprises overlapping cultural conversations, in the details of which viewers recognize or learn about themselves and others—be these suspects shot and dragging themselves through police stations, *Menanti Ajal* with its white piano, a ghost dancing with a house-owner in *Pemburu Hantu*, a Muslim woman's ordeal at a haunted Hindu bathing-place in *Dunia Lain*, or the subsequent vogue for showcasing the poor in programmes such as, for example, *Nikah Gratis* (*Complimentary Wedding*) and *Uang Kaget* (*Surprise Money*). To reduce the complexities of Indonesian class, power and their representation to processes of global capital says relatively little and fails to address how Indonesians articulate their differing relationships to the mass media and the world around them.

Producers and élites may attempt to predetermine or ignore audiences, but it would be a serious failure of critical scholarship were media studies' scholars to collude. Not least in the post-Suharto years, as the role of the mass media—and television in particular—has attained a new importance for reform-minded Indonesians. But how are we to set about thinking about audiences, which have proven so refractory to analysis (Ang, 1991; Hartley, 1992; Morley, 1992)? This is not the place to develop a comprehensive account. However, the programmes discussed above do indicate difficulties with some standard assumptions and suggest interesting alternatives.

Most obviously, should we think of supernatural programmes as popular culture, and so as constituting grounds for 'resistance' to political and economic élites? Remarkably, considering the emancipatory political agenda of most cultural studies' scholars, they have failed to consider the implications. Resistance is a term borrowed from classical mechanics. It is passive and its possibilities are determined by the force that acts upon it. It exemplifies Laclau's (1996) paradox of radical emancipation, for emancipation inevitably bears the traces of what it opposes. Resistance is the slippery path by which intellectuals, however radical-seeming, yet again seek to determine the conditions of their subjects' actions. However, Mini-DV and other inexpensive and accessible technology may well prove emancipatory in unexpected ways as people record and disseminate events, lives and social practices in ways which defy the tight conventions of broadcasting.

If resistance proves too hegemonic a way of addressing audiences' implication in television, are there alternatives? Three suggest themselves. An evident starting point is Baudrillard's (1988) elegant presuppositional critique of how attempts to survey, know and address the masses are doomed to failure, because they misunderstand the nature of their subjects. Baudrillard's account remains however trapped in the metaphysics he himself subverts. It is a brilliant critical analysis which demonstrates the limits of Western thinking, but can offer no alternative. Here the work of Bakhtin is potentially relevant. His analysis of social life as dialogic offers ways of imagining the necessary relevance of audiences to producers without marginalizing or turning them into false positivities (for example, Morson & Emerson, 1990). And Bakhtin's (1984) account of carnival, of a European genealogy of humour and ways of subverting authority, are suggestive. While the parallels are obvious with the comedic and commentative role of servants in Indonesian theatre and now television, there are risks facilely in reading across two such different cultural histories. The risk of discovering yourself and what you want to see in the imagined mirror of the Other is ever-present.

At least partly to circumvent these problems, we may need to adopt more critical anthropological approaches, which were designed to address such traps. Now, as theatre in Indonesia provides a crucial world of pre-understandings which both actors and audiences bring to television, perhaps we should look to work on theatre to appreciate the mutual knowledge which is the necessary condition of viewing. In an important article, Alton Becker (1979) argued that applying European criteria of analysis to Javanese theatre was a fundamental category mistake, because Javanese use a quite different metaphysics of theatre and representation. In place of the unitary epistemology assumed in Western analyses of theatre, Javanese played with distinct epistemologies—feudal, cosmological, sensual, pragmatic and ideological—which cross-cut one another in complex and partly contingent ways. As the pragmatic epistemology of survival runs counter to, and is critical of, the hierarchical epistemology of the ruling élite, little wonder Indonesian élites worry about the subversive possibilities unleashed by television. On this account, the attempts at articulation—and so hegemony—of television as a culture industry are always unfinalizable.

Framed this way, it becomes obvious that mass communications' approaches to non-Western media are of necessity largely restricted to finding the Same in the Other. To recognize the diversity that exists, we have to think in new ways. This is why entertainment is a more fruitful starting point than news and factual broadcasting. These latter are committed to highly questionable—indeed wildly implausible— assumptions about representing reality. The critical study of entertainment points us to the need to recognize heteroglossia, to a world of heterogeneous utterances and irreconcilable subject positions. Otherwise it is not just Indonesian élites but media studies' scholars who are entertaining illusions.

Acknowledgements

My thanks go to Philip Kitley and Richard Fox who, as reviewer and co-editor, respectively, made useful comments on this piece.

Notes

[1] Sen and Hill (2000, pp. 80–107) note the singular liveliness of radio in the late New Order, a vitality which has now spread to the point that conservative groups, notable among them Islamists, are pushing for the reintroduction of censorship, in the guise of anti-pornography laws under discussion in Parliament as I write.

[2] Reputedly, at the time, these were the top rated programmes on terrestrial channels. However, reliable viewing figures are hard to come by from ACNielsen Indonesia or other sources.

[3] Regulation reins in TV content (2006, March 2), *The Jakarta Post*.

[4] Where relevant I shall use the Indonesian terms because they have distinctive senses in Indonesia.

[5] By the summer of 2002, programmes devoted exclusively to crime and violence were already a significant feature of scheduling for the main commercial channels.

[6] Grierson's (1932, p. 8) definition as 'the creative interpretation of actuality' neatly suggests the ambiguity and constructed nature of the genre.

[7] I am referring to who is allowed to speak and say what within highly structured genres, not to what audiences make of the programmes, which is an entirely different matter.

[8] I once remarked on how cooperative the suspects seemed in almost always confessing, until an Indonesian friend kindly pointed out what happened if they did not.

[9] Two series, *Jakarta Underground*, with its spin-off, *The Underground*, both on Lativi, were particularly innovative. While their mainstay was what seemed a rather voyeuristic exploration of prostitution, homosexuality and other previously undiscussable topics, sometimes they offered good coverage of underworld scenes, where people were allowed to talk at length with minimal editing.

[10] Oddly the ghosts often looked like particularly hirsute Dutchmen—an instance of transcendental post-colonialism?

[11] The appearance of realism, as with other genres like hard news, is necessary to disguise the degree to which broadcasters impose cultural conventions upon labile actuality.

[12] *Pornoaksi* is public indecency. I use the Indonesian terms, because their connotations are distinct from the English.

[13] This article is not intended as a survey of Indonesian print media commentary on *kriminal* and *mistik*. So I have not engaged in a detailed analysis of the inflections of coverage over the years across relevant print media. My concern rather is with how politicians, intellectuals and media producers use selected broadsheets to enunciate on such subjects. The two most relevant publications for these purposes are *Kompas*, which is the leading platform for public pronouncements, and *Republika*, which aims to offer a distinctly Islamic voice. Neither newspaper takes a single line; and the differences of accent within and between newspapers is complex and changing. I concentrate on *Kompas* here because there was a long-running intermittent debate about the pernicious effects of television, especially from 2002 onwards.

[14] Articles citing the code of media ethics on 3 February and 1 July 2004.

[15] Unless otherwise stated, all parentheses are mine.

[16] Commercial television and the opinion survey (2003, September 8), *Kompas*.

[17] By contrast Baudrillard once remarked that every time he watched television he was a member of the masses. After all, by definition, it is a mass medium.

[18] That is, it mocks the existing order of power and constitutes the antithesis of production, accumulation and privilege.

References

Andrejevic, M. (2004). *Reality TV: The work of being watched*. Oxford: Rowman & Littlefield.

Ang, I. (1991). *Desperately seeking the audience*. London: Routledge.

Bakhtin, M. M. (1981). Forms of time in the chronotope of the novel. In M. Holquist (Ed.), *The dialogic imagination: Four essays* (C. Emerson & M. Holquist, Trans.). Austin: University of Texas Press.

Bakhtin, M. M. (1984). *Rabelais and his world* (H. Iswolsky, Trans.). Bloomington: Indiana University Press.

Baudrillard, J. (1988). The masses: The implosion of the social in the media. In M. Poster (Ed.), *Jean Baudrillard: Selected writings* (M. Maclean, Trans.). Oxford: Polity.

Baudrillard, J. (1990). *Seduction* (B. Singer, Trans.). New York: St. Martin's Press.

Becker, A. L. (1979). Text-building, epistemology and aesthetics in Javanese shadow theatre. In A. L. Becker, & A. A. (Eds.), *The imagination of reality: Essays in Southeast Asian coherence systems*. Norwood, NJ: Ablex.

Brenton, S., & Cohen, R. (2003). *Shooting people: Adventures in reality TV*. London: Verso.

Collingwood, R. G. (1940). *An essay on metaphysics*. Oxford: Clarendon Press.

Dyer, R. (1992). *Only entertainment*. London: Routledge.

Ellis, J. (1992). *Visible fictions* (Rev. ed.). London: Routledge & Kegan Paul.

Fiske, J., & Hartley, J. (1978). *Reading television*. London: Methuen.

Foucault, M. (1977). *Discipline and punish: The birth of the prison* (A. Sheridan, Trans.). Harmondsworth: Penguin.

Grierson, J. (1932). The documentary producer. *Cinema Quarterly*, 2, 145–153.

Hartley, J. (1992). *Tele-ology: Studies in television*. London: Routledge.

Holmes, S., & Jermyn, D. (Eds.). (2004). *Understanding reality television*. London: Routledge.

Kilborn, R. (2003). *Staging the real: Factual TV programming in the age of Big Brother*. Manchester: University Press.

Laclau, E. (1996). Beyond emancipation. In *Emancipation(s)*. London: Verso.

Morley, D. (1992). *Television, audiences and cultural studies*. London: Routledge.

Morson, G. S., & Emerson, C. (1990). *Mikhail Bakhtin: Creation of a prosaics*. Stanford, CA: University Press.

Nilai Tayangan Program Mistik di Televisi Terpulang ke Pemirsa (2003, August 27). *Kompas*.

'Pendapat Kompas' Menenggak Mimpi dan Kekerasan dari Sajian Televisi (2003, August 25). *Kompas*.

Perilaku Dipengaruhi Keseringan Nonton Televisi (2002, July 26). *Kompas*.

Poster, M. (1990). *The mode of information: Poststructuralism and social context*. Oxford: Polity.

Salahuddin, W. (2003, April 16). HAM dan Berita Kriminalitas. *Kompas*.

Sen, K., & &. Hill, D. T. (2000). *Media, culture, and politics in Indonesia*. South Melbourne: Oxford University Press.

Tayangan Mistik di Televisi Tumpulkan Logika (2003, August 26). *Kompas*.

Televisi Swasta dan Jajak Pendapat (2003, September 8). *Kompas*.

Tema Misteri Cermin Kegundahan (2003, March 5). *Kompas*.

Dangdut Soul: Who are 'the People' in Indonesian Popular Music?

Andrew N. Weintraub

In a 1979 article published in the music magazine *Aktuil*, cultural critic and poet Emha Ainun Nadjib (Emha) admonished Indonesians for losing their collective 'dangdut soul' (Emha, 1979). Dangdut, a genre of Indonesian popular music associated with urban underclass audiences, was often represented in the pages of *Aktuil* and other popular print media of the period as backward, hickish, and unsophisticated (*kampungan*).[1] Writing for an educated middle class and elite readership hailed by Western narratives of modernity (*modernitas*), Emha noted that, despite their desire to progress (*maju*), all Indonesians are 'very dangdut' (*dangdut sekali*). As transnational products flooded the Indonesian market, Emha asked, 'what are we if not a bunch of brown-skinned western clothes-wearing people with a dangdut mentality?'

Emha never defined precisely what he meant by 'dangdut soul', or 'dangdut mentality', although he insisted that all Indonesians possessed these attributes. He used dangdut as a space to expose the hypocrisy of elite society and to reflect on definitions of progress associated with Suharto's New Order regime, namely, Western-style capitalism, intensified commodification, and a culture of consumerism. Modernity might look good on the outside, but it disguised the everyday problems that faced most Indonesians, and it threatened to exacerbate social inequalities. Emha's impassioned critique urged readers to take a hard look at their own cultural history, a strategy employed by dangdut songs but not by songs in other popular music genres including jazz and pop Indonesia. By looking inward, another classic move associated with dangdut, Emha urged Indonesians to reflect on their own lives, and on the lives of people around them, rather than outward toward the West.

Almost 30 years later, dangdut—Indonesia's most popular music—can be heard blaring out of speakers on public concert stages and in homes, narrow alleyways, roadside food stalls, karaoke bars, hotels, stores, restaurants, and all forms of public transportation.[2] In the 1990s, among all genres of Indonesian music tracked by ASIRI, the Indonesian Sound Recording Industry Association, about 35% of music recording sales was dangdut (Sen & Hill, 2000, p. 170). In 2006, an informal survey of weekly television programming showed that 29 out of 43 music programs were devoted exclusively to dangdut (67%), while another poll showed that dangdut could be viewed on television 566.5 minutes per day and 3965 minutes per week.[3]

This essay is an ideological critique of popular print media about dangdut, primarily focusing on media constructions of the people who constitute its audience. The audience for dangdut has been imagined, represented, and mobilized in various ways to support the ideological interests of commercial, government, and critical institutions. Using an historical approach, I construct an interpretation of these representational practices, taking into account shifts in the social meaning and function of dangdut's audience.[4]

Representations of dangdut as the music of 'the people' (*rakyat*)—the majority of society—have been produced with great frequency and in a variety of popular print media. 'The people' is not a singular unified category, and neither is dangdut's audience, but the term signifies the juxtaposition of class and nation that characterizes the discourse about dangdut.[5] Dangdut is thought to reflect the desires and aspirations of 'the people', primarily those who occupy the lower stratum of the political and economic structure: 'little people' (*rakyat kecil*); 'common people' (*rakyat jelata*); 'poverty-stricken' (*rakyat jémbél*); 'underclass group' (*golongan bawah*); 'marginalized group' (*kaum marginal*); those who have been pushed aside (*pinggiran*); and 'the middle class and below' (*kelas menengah ke bawah*).

In the late 1980s, the shape of the dangdut audience began to change. Formerly associated with the disenfranchised and depoliticized underclass, the music began to appeal to middle class and elite audiences as well.[6] Dangdut extended its reach into middle class living rooms via commercial television in the early 1990s. This shift in social geography, signified by dangdut's popularity with the masses *and* the middle classes, placed dangdut in a powerful social position. The notion that dangdut represented the 'soul of the Indonesian people', together with its massive popularity, engendered a discourse about music and national identification among top government and military officials. Sung in lyrics that nearly all Indonesians could understand, expressing feelings that nearly everyone could relate to, and with a beat that everyone could dance to, it was not surprising, so the argument goes, that dangdut had become Indonesia's national music. Dangdut's representation and meaning changed from the music of the common people who occupy the bottom of the political system, to a genre celebrated as national music by military and government officials in the 1990s, to a large consumer industry in the 21st century. I contend that the middle classes and elites had long participated in dangdut as a discursive practice, if only as a way to distance themselves from the people and culture associated with dangdut. While dangdut's audience has certainly grown, I remain skeptical that dangdut has been thoroughly incorporated into the national culture of Indonesia, as claimed by government and military officials in popular print media.

In this essay, I describe the ways in which popular print media 'speaks for' people, and the relations of power that define those discourses. Dangdut's audience only comes into focus through representation, and it is largely absent as the author of its own representation. In this way, popular print media play a large role in shaping what it is possible to think and know about 'the people'. I concentrate on the ways in which stories about 'the people' have been narrated and mobilized within a discourse about music in popular print media. What kind of story has been told about 'the people' through dangdut in popular print media? How are they called into being by these stories? Where and when are they represented? For what purposes are they invoked?

Rather than producing a structural homology between Indonesian society and music, in which a type of music reflects the interests of a class, I contend that dangdut as a discursive practice has actively participated in shaping meanings about 'the people'. Dangdut's audience did not exist prior to the creation of dangdut, as a group whose class interests were subsequently reflected in a musical genre.[7] Dangdut does not belong to a class, as a category or attribute of that class. Rather, dangdut acts as a structuring agent that helps to produce meanings about 'the people' in Indonesian society.

The history of dangdut is also the history of its telling. I take an historical approach to show how representations and meanings of dangdut's audience have changed. It is important to specify when, where, and under what social conditions dangdut came to be represented as the music of 'the people'. By taking this approach, I seek to provide a critical understanding of Indonesian media and its construction of popular music audiences within the changing social and historical conditions of modern Indonesia.

Dangdut

Dangdut is a genre of mass-mediated popular music that developed in the Indonesian capital city of Jakarta during the early 1970s. Indonesia's most popular music is arguably its most hybrid, blending Melayu, Arabic, and Indian musical elements with American, Latin, and European popular forms.[8] Within the multi-ethnic, multi-lingual, and multi-cultural context of Jakarta, dangdut gave people a common 'language' that helped them forge a common culture.

The basic instrumentation consists of guitar, bass, drums, electronic keyboard, mandolin, and tambourine, as well as two instruments that give dangdut its distinctive sound: *gendang* (a set of two drums similar to a north Indian *tabla*) and *suling* (transverse flute). Rhoma Irama, dangdut's most important artist, crystallized the form and popularized the music through live concerts and recordings in the 1970s. Rhoma Irama's lyrics expressed themes of everyday life, love, social criticism against class inequality, and Islamic messages (Frederick, 1982). Dangdut also enjoys regional popularity in live performances at weddings, circumcisions, and other events hosted by individuals or community groups. In live concerts, the performers dance in comic or sexually suggestive ways, while mostly male audiences dance themselves into 'a state where they [are] unaware of their surroundings, free of self-consciousness and inhibition' (Yampolsky, 1991, p. 1). Female fans of dangdut enjoy the music at home via musical recordings and music television programs.[9]

The notion of dangdut *as* the music of the people (*musik rakyat*) has been a common theme since the genre's inception in the early 1970s. Rhoma Irama, the primary force behind the development of dangdut, states that 'the name "dangdut" is actually an insulting term used by "the haves" toward the music of the poor neighborhoods [where it originated]. They ridiculed the sound of the drum, the dominant element in Orkes Melayu [one of dangdut's musical precursors]. Then we threw the insult right back via a song, which we named "Dangdut"'[10] ('Berjuang dalam goyang', 1989, p. 17). This connection to the *rakyat* persists to the present day. Dangdut's popularity, and the articulation of dangdut with the *rakyat*, is based on its: (1) roots in the melodies, rhythms, and vocal style of Melayu popular music (*orkes melayu*); (2) Indonesian-language lyrics; (3) relatively simple style of dance (*joget* and *goyang*); (4) straightforward and easily comprehensible lyrics; and (5) texts which deal with everyday realities of ordinary people.

Dangdut's growing popularity in the late 1970s had as much to do with the creative activity of influential innovative artists and new socioeconomic realities, as it did with the nature of its musical origins, texts, and style of dance. Rhoma Irama's populist messages and danceable beat appealed to an urban, mostly male, underclass audience. New flows of transnational capital were used to establish infrastructures of media communications that allowed the music to be broadcast on radio and television; new electronic technologies enabled the music to travel in the form of cassette recordings and films to regions far from the urban capital; new forms of promotion and publicity including films, billboards, and magazines, generated interest in the social lives of entertainers and celebrities; and a new ethos of consumerism in Indonesia gave people the motivation to buy commercial products associated with popular music.

Dangdut's popularity was based on its ability to adapt to different circumstances and conditions. As one dangdut fan told me, 'there is a dangdut song for every social situation' (E. Rumbini, personal communication, 20 March 2006). As commercial music, it has had to adapt to changing markets, media, and technologies. Songs were created for particular audiences in particular places, and address themes that other genres avoid (Mansyur S., quoted in Aribowo, 2002) including drunkenness and gambling ('Mabuk dan Judi'); leaving a love behind ('Aduh Buyung'); living in poverty ('Gubuk Derita'); finding a man with another woman ('Rambut'); and prostitution ('Hitam Duniamu Putih Cintaku'). Titles of songs reveal the range of everyday issues addressed in dangdut: 'The poorest in the world' ('Termiskin di Dunia'); 'Sterility' ('Mandul'); 'Homelessness' ('Gelandangan'); 'Liar' ('Dusta'); 'Suffering on top of suffering' ('Derita di atas Derita'); and 'Crazy for Divorced Women' ('Mabuk Janda').

1979: The Day of the Dang Duts

In newspaper and magazine articles of the 1970s that most dangdut fans would never read, sandwiched between advertisements for products that most dangdut fans would never consume, were stories about dangdut singers, concerts, recordings, and fans themselves. The consumers of these magazine and newspaper articles were not the fans of the music; rather, dangdut stood for the masses 'out there'. In these stories, middle class and elite readers of newspapers and magazines positioned themselves in relation to dangdut's underclass audience. The masses that constituted dangdut's audience were generally imagined in a negative light as uneducated, ignorant, and irrational. They were incapable of acting together in an organized way; rather than acting, they were acted upon as objects that could be read about in popular print media. When they did become active, at concerts, for example, they were accused of being unruly and violent.

News magazine *Tempo* labeled 1979 'the year of dangdut' and published the first historical account of the genre in a cover story entitled 'The day of the dang duts' (5 May 1979). The feature article focused on the rising popularity of dangdut, which had begun to challenge the dominance of pop Indonesia, a genre of music largely oriented toward 'the middle class and above'. As a result, a few pop singers made efforts to cross over to dangdut to capitalize on its market success. Popular print media emphasized the schism between pop Indonesia and dangdut, whose audience was 'the middle class and below'. Pop singers distinguished themselves by their inability to sing dangdut, as if it were a foreign style ('Dangdut, setelah halal di TV-RI', 1979).

Some producers believed that the popularity of dangdut was rising because the popularity of pop Indonesia was falling. But pop stars interviewed for the 1979 *Tempo* article had different opinions on the matter. Titiek Puspa noted that pop singers only sang dangdut because producers wanted them to. She noted that it would be much more difficult for a dangdut singer to sing pop than for a pop singer to sing dangdut, because dangdut was closer to the people. For Titiek Puspa, dangdut required a different kind of feeling (*penjiwaan*). Chrisye loved dangdut, but did not feel he could sing it. Franky of Franky and Jane was also not interested and remained loyal to *lagu country* (American-inspired folk songs). Bob Tutupoly and Grace Simon (who sang a dangdut song in 1973 that did not become popular) thought that dangdut was fine, but was just having its day (as they had their day). For Melky Goeslaw, being a Christian made it hard to sing dangdut because its melodies came from India and its rhythms and vocal style were close to Arabic-influenced forms like *gambus* and *qasidah*, especially the ornaments in the vocal part. Jazz artist Jack Lesmana felt that pop singers could not possibly be successful as artists in the dangdut style, so it was solely a matter of their wanting to be commercially successful that drove their participation in dangdut.

In general, commentary by pop stars tended to focus on dangdut as a commodity form, and they downplayed its aesthetic and social value. For pop singers, dangdut was even more foreign than American music. Further, dangdut did not signify prestige or progress. As musician and author Remy Sylado observed, 'Dangdut always looks to the past. With Pop, its orientation is to America' ('Goyang dangdut', 1991, p. 53). And, as singer Titiek Puspa noted, dangdut was too close to 'the people'.

Dangdut's relationship with Indonesian Rock was similarly class-inflected. In the 1970s, *Aktuil* featured articles on dangdut as part of its broader reportage on Indonesian popular music. *Aktuil*, as described on the magazine's credits page (p. 137), was a 'magazine for youth as well as those who are young at heart'. Published from 1967 to 1981, the magazine featured stories about bands, interviews, concert reviews, and advertisements for jeans, sunglasses, and other accessories of a modern lifestyle. Each issue included a full-color fold-out poster of bands including Led Zeppelin and Deep Purple as well as Indonesian groups including God Bless and Giant Step. Editors at Aktuil reportedly coined the term 'dangdut' as a derogatory label for the music's characteristic and persistent drum pattern 'dang-dut'.[11]

Aktuil had a love–hate relationship with dangdut in its depiction of singers and audiences.[12] The rock contingent, most of them teenagers from middle class and elite families, identified symbolically with dangdut's disruption of proper social behavior. For example, dangdut fans were depicted as explosive, raging, and wild (*membludag*) and fans were portrayed as belonging to 'dangdut gangs' (Miloer, 1978, p. 53). But the rock audience could not quite accept the rough vocal style of dangdut singers, the garishness of dangdut's fashions, or its concert etiquette. Female dangdut singers were ridiculed for wearing short skirts and high boots that stretched up to the knees. Singers 'screamed' songs rather than sang them. For rock audiences of the period, music was something that should be listened to and appreciated for its sound. Describing the audience at one concert, the author wrote: 'the scene was truly wild ... it was such a shame that the audience couldn't just sit and enjoy the show and appeared so unruly' (Miloer, 1978, p. 53). Unfortunately, the author missed the point that a dangdut audience dressed and behaved differently from a rock audience. For example, dangdut audiences moved their bodies during a show rather than listening intently to the music and applauding after each song.

During the 1970s, dangdut was broadcast on television, but it was portrayed as a subcategory of pop and not seriously considered in its own right (Soemardi, 1979). The first television programs specifically geared to dangdut did not feature popular dangdut artists, but rather university-based dangdut groups from the prestigious University of Indonesia and Gadjah Mada University. Although dangdut exerted a notable presence in middle class and elite media, the voices of dangdut artists and audiences were absent. On television, they were replaced by university students playing humorous versions of dangdut songs (Simatupang, 1996).

Dangdut was placed in relation to other competing genres of popular music in order to make distinctions among different classes of people. These articles helped to define notions of *kampungan*—'backward', represented by people who listen to dangdut—and *gedongan*—'progressive', as in those who listen to other kinds of music, namely, pop Indonesia and rock. In the pages of print media, dangdut became a social text for assigning all sorts of meanings—*kampungan*, for example—through which elites could register their own class position. Despite the fact that elites were not the target audience of the music, dangdut became both a sign and a target of essentialist elite constructions of Indonesian identity.

Dangdut and New Order Censorship

Popular print media emphasized distancing between readers and dangdut audiences to create distinctions between social classes. But this was not the only representation available to the readers of popular print magazines and newspapers. As dangdut's popularity grew, it generated a variety of attitudes about the genre's meaning and function. Dangdut's popularity made it particularly ripe for constructing a discourse about music and Indonesian national identity in the 1980s (Aribowo, 1983; 'Satria berdakwah', 1984).

Populist messages resonated with the majority of society, but they conflicted with the aims of the authoritarian Suharto regime. Benedict Anderson (1990) writes that the *rakyat* have long been perceived as a central symbol of Indonesian nationalism, but they were '*masih bodoh*' ('still stupid', ignorant, and unformed). Dangdut fans, synonymous with the masses, were discursively produced in popular print media according to middle class and elite notions of the *rakyat* as explosive and uncontrolled. But through censorship, the hickish and uninformed could be transformed into national subjects.

The top–down approach to culture was carried out within other media, notably the state television network TVRI (Kitley, 2000). TVRI targeted those who watched television—middle classes and elites, not the majority of society—and programming followed its audience's desires. Dangdut artists were featured regularly on the TVRI music television show called Aneka Ria Safari, but dangdut was not promoted on any other shows. Dangdut's most influential artist, Rhoma Irama, was banned from performing on TVRI from 1977 to 1988. TVRI and the state-run radio network RRI refused to play Rhoma Irama's music, including songs 'Rupiah' ('Money') and 'Hak Azasi' ('Human rights') because they threatened to expose social problems, which, according to the Department of Information, would subsequently ignite audiences, and destabilize the government (which, of course, only fueled Rhoma Irama's popularity and sales of recordings). During the early 1980s, dangdut became a symbol of resistance against the New Order military regime (Barraud, 2003). From 1977 to 1982, Rhoma Irama aligned himself with the Islamic Opposition Party (PPP) against Suharto's ruling government group (Golkar), and this led to state media censorship of his music (Sen & Hill, 2000). News magazine *Tempo* reported that Rhoma Irama was banned from TVRI in 1977 because of a contractual dispute with recording company Remaco, which had strong ties to TVRI's dangdut program 'Mana Suka' ('Hak Asasi Dilarang', 1977, p. 17). Rhoma Irama was told that the reason for the banning was due to the use of the *gendang*, a set of two drums used in dangdut. Rhoma Irama stated that '[i]n 1977 (last year) we did not yet have democracy. Just look at the TVRI regulations in which a drum kit has to be used in dangdut … gendang is not allowed. What is so sinful about gendang?' ('Dua orang raja', 1978, p. 42.).

This pattern of state censorship illustrates the construction of dangdut's audience as an object of a top–down New Order discourse about culture and the arts in the 1980s characterized by government regulation and monitoring (Lindsay, 1995; Yampolsky, 1995; Zurbuchen, 1990). As Yampolsky (1989) and Williams (1989) have shown for pop Indonesia and pop Sunda, respectively, publicly voicing everyday problems in popular music was not good for Indonesia, according to New Order officials, especially if the songs were mournful (*cengeng*) or eroticized (*porno*).[13] The music of the 1980s was anything but light popular fare. Rather, there was a great deal of cultural politics around the lyrics, which reflected on poverty, unemployment, loss, and despair. Dangdut was especially vulnerable to these charges as its settings and themes emerge out of people's everyday lives.

Populist Chic

In popular print media of the 1980s, it became trendy to use dangdut as part of a discourse about Indonesian national character. William Frederick (1982), describing Rhoma Irama's music, noted the fascination with dangdut:

> In the eyes of many observers, the music not only gets the majority of its fans from the majority of society—the lower classes—but evinces a sympathy with and

understanding of them that is unique. Indeed, this last characteristic has been strong enough to breed a kind of 'populist chic' (*kegenitan sosial*) among the elite and middle class. For these reasons some have concluded that the dangdut style, by virtue of what it reflects as well as what it imposes, matches more accurately than any other yet devised the much sought-after national character or 'countenance'. (p. 124)

Rhoma Irama's music *reflected* 'an Indonesian flavor, free from foreign influence—at least an Eastern sound' ('Satria berdakwah', 1984, p. 30). His songs *imposed* uplifting populist messages about human rights ('Hak Azasi'), staying up all night ('Begadang'), social equality ('Termenung'), and social struggle through Islam ('Perjuangan dan Do'a'). And Rhoma Irama's dangdut films depict a 'cross-class success story in which the underdog wins against all odds' (Frederick, 1982, p. 115). These qualities elicited sympathy among middle classes and elites.

Yet, the emotionally excessive, overblown, and extreme nature of dangdut would have to be tempered in order for dangdut to be fully integrated as part of the Indonesian national character. In a 1987 issue of *Mutiara*, a glossy fashion magazine, dangdut music was described as 'unsophisticated, weak, tacky, and whimpering' ('Rhoma Irama', 1987, p. 21). In another magazine, fans were described as 'hysterical' (*histeris*) ('Berjuang dalam goyang', 1989, p. 13). These characterizations were sure to attract middle class and elite readers of magazines. But rather than simply denigrating the music as '*kampungan*', as had numerous other articles, the author found a redemptive quality in dangdut: 'Dangdut is not just light entertainment to pass the time, but it can be considered a tool for expression, an instrument to express the culture of the people' ('Rhoma Irama', 1987, p. 21). The article cited interviews with university faculty experts from the arts and sciences. Drs. Ryadi Gunawan, a member of the literature faculty at Gadjah Mada University, called Rhoma Irama's music a 'social barometer' (p. 22). Drs. Hasan Basri from the Psychology Department at the same university depicted Rhoma Irama's music as a form of psychotherapy (p. 22). According to Dr. Lukman Sutrisno, whose affiliation was not cited, dangdut served a positive role in society, but only because of its ability to 'repress' (*meredam*) feelings of frustration among its audiences (p. 22). And Dr. Kuntowijoyo, an historian and cultural expert, noted that Rhoma Irama's songs could 'sublimate' (*mensublimasi*) social protest through culture and the arts (pp. 22, 23).

Another article represented the populist chic attitude in a way that suggested a deeper understanding and appreciation of the music (Suyitno, 1991, p. 33). In an article entitled 'Dangdut music and its excesses', Drs. Ayid Suyitno wrote that 'as people with a culture, we should be proud of the strength of dangdut on our native soil' (p. 33). The author quite accurately summarized the lyrics of dangdut songs as follows:

> ... there is an honesty and openness difficult to find in other forms of Indonesian popular music. Don't be alarmed by hearing about a 'shot-gun wedding;' 'a divorcee's heartache;' 'a husband has another lover;' 'true love doesn't value material circumstances'. (p. 33)

Dangdut's strength lay in its ability to express the emotional realities of ordinary people. But according to the article, its messages were being diverted (*diselewengkan*) by singers' inability to speak the language properly, and the vulgar quality of 'overacting' by performers and audiences. Unless properly transformed, the style of its delivery would forever doom dangdut to reside among the lower classes in Jakarta's slums:

> I'm sorry, but the words are extremely vulgar, inaccurate, and not particularly intelligent. This may constitute one of the strongest arguments for proving that dangdut is only appropriate for the lower class, and moreover points to its vileness. (p. 33)

Despite the author's familiarity with dangdut's lyrical content and its high level of emotional expression, the article represents a contradiction that is difficult to resolve. Dangdut's ability to communicate honestly and openly with its audience was grounded in a particular style of language ('vulgar, inaccurate, and not particularly intelligent') and performance ('overacting'), yet these linguistic and performative qualities were marked as responsible for diverting its messages. Cleaning up the language of dangdut, and transforming the way people respond (by 'acting' but not 'overacting'), would somehow enable dangdut fans to improve the social and economic conditions of their lives. In this text, as in the preceding example, dangdut could only be appreciated when it was *not* dangdut, and its fans could only be valued when their desires and behaviors were repressed, sublimated, or otherwise transformed.

1991: 'Of the People, By the People, For the People'

The discourse about dangdut in popular print media changed in the early 1990s. As the country moved toward its 50th anniversary, dangdut was promoted as the music for *all* Indonesians. In 1991, *Tempo* proclaimed that dangdut had quietly risen in social status and was no longer simply the music of the lower class ('Goyang dangdut', 1991, p. 49): 'Bureaucrats, from government ministers up to the vice governor—and quite likely many others—have begun to admit they like dangdut'. Dangdut reached new audiences by splintering off into subgenres including *disko dangdut* and *dangdut trendy*, which blended dangdut with musical styles and production techniques heard in middle class and elite entertainment venues.

Several factors led to this shift in the discourse about dangdut, as its image in popular print media changed from music for the underclass to music for everyone. Newly formed national dangdut organizations, supported by the national government, sponsored singing competitions. There were numerous articles about whether dangdut's origins were rooted more deeply in Melayu music ('us'), or whether it was based more heavily on Indian film music ('them'), and Melayu was clearly the privileged category of influence ('Pedoman dangdut berasal dari Melayu', 1994, p. 4).

In the 1980s, dangdut was still the 'poor stepchild' of pop Indonesia but sales figures printed in *Tempo* in 1992 demonstrated that dangdut was gaining the upper hand ('Dangdut goyang', 1992, p. 108). Dangdut was more profitable than pop because the cost of producing a pop album was more expensive than a dangdut album, and dangdut cassettes were therefore cheaper to buy ('Dangdut goyang', 1992, p. 108). As a result, pop singers (Chrisye, Trio Libels, Ruth Sahanaya) began crossing over to dangdut. Recordings by pop singers who had not crossed over (Jamal Mirdad, Denny Malik, Hetty Koes Endang) were put on hold ('Dangdut goyang', 1992, p. 108). This period marks a difference from the late 1970s, where dangdut was regarded as difficult to sing and too close to 'the people'. As the demand for dangdut increased, and the profits increased, pop singers were more willing to cross over.

The promotion of dangdut as Indonesia's national music encountered resistance from TVRI, the national television network. Although TVRI programmed five dangdut shows at the national level (*Aneka Ria Safari*, *Aneka Ria Safari Nusantara*, *Irama Masa Kini*, *Kamera Ria*, *Album Minggu*, and *Panggung Hiburan Anak-Anak*), there were limits on the amount of dangdut programming allowed on TVRI. 'The percentage of dangdut on Aneka Ria Safari can be up to 50 percent, and on Ablum Minggu it can be up to 40 percent', said Hoediono Drajat, Director of Planning for Music and Entertainment at TVRI Jakarta ('Goyang dangdut', 1991, p. 50). There was also local programming of dangdut; for example, on TVRI Medan (Sumatra), a show called *Arena Ria*, modeled on *Aneka Ria Safari*, featured 50% dangdut (p. 50). A year later, TVRI surpassed these limits: 'Dangdut shows are not allowed more than 30% [on music programs]. As it turns out, dangdut dominates with almost 75% of music programs. "Dangdut is now the trend. We are satisfying the tastes of the people", said Hoediono' ('Dangdut goyang', 1992, p. 108).

TVRI exerted strict controls over what could be shown. Songs were banned for allegedly creating a bad image of Indonesia, including 'Are you a virgin or not' ('Gadis atau Janda?') and 'Grilled corn' ('Jagung Bakar') both banned from being shown on TVRI in early 1992 ('Penayangan dangdut', 1992). The reasons for controlling content were not clear. Dangdut fans reportedly complained about the lyrics and erotic movements on television ('Giliran musik dangdut', 1992). But the government did not have a mechanism to identify the people's wishes. In the case of 'Are you a virgin or not?' it seems more likely that the state censorship board denounced the depiction of a woman who was in control of her own body, especially if that woman were sexually active with more than one person.

The emergence of commercial television in the early 1990s changed the face of music (Sutton, 2003). TVRI broadcast dangdut, but its programming was limited and its content was controlled. Deregulation of the television industry encouraged diversity of programming and an emphasis on entertainment (Kitley, 2000). Airtime on the private stations could be bought relatively cheaply, compared to TVRI. In the early 1990s, through the commercial stations, dangdut became a commodity that could be sold to sponsors. Dangdut's established audience began watching more television and the private stations began to cater to this growing market of potential consumers of products advertised during dangdut programs.

The relationship between dangdut and the New Order state was particularly focused and concentrated, garnering close attention in the popular print media.[14] Major New Order figures involved in dangdut included Basofi Sudirman; Siti Hardiyanti Rukmana (Suharto's eldest daughter and the main shareholder of television station TPI); B.J. Habibie, Minister of State for Research and Technology; and Moerdiono, Secretary of State, among others. In the New Order newspaper *Pos Kota*, Habibie and Moerdiono were shown dancing dangut at a rally in May 1992, urging the crowd to vote in an upcoming Golkar regional election in June ('Moerdiono dan Habibie', 1992).

Quotes by high-ranking ministers assimilated dangdut to the slogan-laden language of New Order politics. Basofi Sudirman claimed that 'with dangdut we will success-ify development' ('Basofi Sudirman', 1994, p. 2). Another 1994 article, entitled 'Pesta Demokrasi Praktisi Dangdut Mencari Figur Pemimpin', compared the search for a new leader of a dangdut organization with the New Order's quinquennial 'festival of democracy' (*pesta demokrasi*) (Harahap, 1994, p. 5). Secretary of State Moerdiono called dangdut a 'commodity with potential for unlimited development ... [and] a chance to go international' in the 1990s (Piper, 1995, p. 44).

Based on governmental, commercial, and critical support for dangdut, and publications about dangdut's heightened presence on television and in elite entertainment venues, it is tempting to argue that dangdut had finally become accepted among all Indonesians as 'our national music'. However, this position ignores the ideological functioning of print media and television, which do not simply reflect social reality but construct it for their own ideological and commercial purposes. It is worth examining in more detail the ideological content and function of these media. Some of them, like the newspaper *Pos Kota*, emphasized the close links between the New Order and dangdut, while others, like news magazine *Tempo*, presented a more critical perspective.

In 1991, *Tempo* published an extensive feature article about the wealth and status of dangdut stars that underscored the widening gap between performers and audiences ('Goyang dangdut', 1991, p. 55). Whereas they used to earn only enough for 'two to eat from one plate' (after the song 'Sepiring Berdua'), now they have enough to 'buy two cars apiece' ('*dua mobil seorang*'). The article stated that 'In dangdut—that *kampungan* form—we not only hear the sound of the drum, but also the sound of a cash register ringing' ('Goyang dangdut', 1991, p. 60).

Tempo used the confluence of dangdut and the New Order as a way to express a position critical of the state ('Goyang dangdut', 1991, p. 55). Secretary of State Moerdiono reportedly loved dangdut, which he listened to as he was being chauffeured to extravagant state functions in his expensive Volvo B-50. Based on an interview with the Secretary of State, the article highlights the incongruity of dangdut representing a high government official:

> 'The words to those kinds of songs can make us more empathetic toward each other', he said to TEMPO female reporter Linda Djalil. 'I feel represented by those words', said Moerdiono. He did not elaborate on what he meant by 'represent', let's

> not forget that he is certainly not someone who 'eats from a shared plate'. What is clear is that his driver put his tape collection together. 'He is the one I order to buy cassettes'. ('Goyang dangdut', 1991, p. 55)

Moerdiono's remarks suggest that dangdut could miraculously become the great equalizer, a medium to erase social inequalities of class, gender, and ethnicity. Moerdiono does not explain what he means by 'represent', suggesting a statement that he cannot support. The author immediately highlights the odd notion that Moerdiono could possibly be represented in a song about not having enough to eat. Further, if he has to send someone else out to choose the music that he reportedly loves, then how much can he actually know about dangdut?

Dangdut was not only a tool for the government to gather the support of 'the people', but it could also be a way for media institutions to mount a critique of the New Order. *Tempo* editor Goenawan Mohamad offered this interpretation in a conversation with me:

> Moerdiono's love for dangdut has to be viewed within the context of the relationship between Moerdiono and [Minister of Information] Harmoko, who had banned dangdut from being shown on TVRI. They were political rivals, although both belonged to the Suharto regime, and they did things behind the scenes. (G. Mohamad, personal communication, 2 July 2006)

Tempo was famous for inserting hidden messages into its reports, especially when quoting high-ranking government officials (Steele, 2005). By affirming that he liked dangdut, Moerdiono sent a signal of his dislike of Harmoko, the Minister of Information who sanctioned the banning of dangdut on TVRI. Moerdiono expressed a position against Harmoko on practically every political issue, mostly in a covert way. The relationship between Moerdiono and Harmoko characterized the inner party conflicts within the New Order regime, which was far from being a monolithic entity. *Tempo* used Moerdiono's dislike of Harmoko, which was veiled in Moerdiono's support for dangdut, to promote its own critique of the New Order regime. In the hands of *Tempo*'s editors, Moerdiono's identification with dangdut became a tool to expand the wedge between two of the New Order's top political strategists. *Tempo*'s publishing license would be revoked three years later under an order from the Department of Information, and Harmoko was suspected of being the mastermind behind the banning of *Tempo* (Steele, 2005).

Another view posits that the music was simply being co-opted for the purposes of attracting the people's support, especially during election times. Not only does this position miss the kind of inner party rivalries discussed above, but it overstates the relative autonomy of social classes and emphasizes too closely the structural homology between commercial music and 'a' class. Dangdut has been a commercial music since its inception in the 1970s, part of an industry that involved 'big bosses' (*tauke*), taste makers, and commercial media tie-ins (Frederick, 1982, p. 125). Clearly, dangdut was a middle class and elite concern, demonstrated by the number of articles in popular print media, as early as the 1970s. The middle and upper classes were missing in these articles as the objects of representation, but they were in fact the ones producing and consuming these commentaries. As the dangdut industry grew in the 1990s, dangdut signified profitability for the private television shareholders, music industry executives, cassette producers, and artists. Ties between government and mass media allowed certain popular forms to flourish, namely those produced in industries with strong government connections (e.g. television).

Going International

In the April 1991 issue of the tabloid *Nova*, 'Kopi Dangdut' was celebrated as the fourth most popular album in Japan, demonstrating dangdut's global market strength, and promoting national pride in the music at home ('Lagi ngetrend', 1991, p. 10). The campaign to 'go international' was not only a way to strengthen dangdut's reputation as Indonesia's national music, but it could be used to dispel its image as *kampungan*: 'It cannot be considered "*kampungan*" anymore because it has already gone international' ('Dangdut menggoyang dunia', 1999, p. 5). No longer content to stay where it was, these sources reported, dangdut was on the move. The headlines declared that 'dangdut had climbed up to the summit' in the late 1990s (Yurnaldi & Rakaryan, 1997). Dangdut was for everyone, from those at the bottom of the political system, to those at the top. Better yet, dangdut could even function as 'aspirin' (*obat pusing*) to cure the country's social ills, which were considerable after the Asian economic crisis in 1997, when the following article was published:

> Dangdut has become the glue that holds together our nation's social classes. As 'aspirin', it can be enjoyed by shoe polishers, newspaper sellers, hard laborers, chauffeurs, housewives, and up to governors and government ministers. ('Generasi baru', 1997)

Yet, what ideas, images, and meanings about the people via dangdut actually appear in popular print media and on television in the late 1990s? Images and stories related to dangdut became even further removed from most people's everyday lives. Pictures and stories about the glamorous lives of dangdut celebrities flooded the tabloid market. Stars were shown performing in sparkling television studios or on spectacular concert stages; dressed in jeans and sportswear at home enjoying their vast leisure time with family; or driving expensive cars, dressed in brand-name clothes, and sitting in cafes with fellow celebrities. One exception was the 1995 TPI program *Dangdut Siang Bolong* shot on location in 'dirty housing developments bordering the marketplace and motorcycle stands and crowded living conditions' of Jakarta ('Dangdut siang bolong', 1995).

As Suharto's New Order regime gasped for breath in mid-1997, the television station TPI sponsored an awards show entitled *Anugerah Dangdut 97*. The award for 'Dangdut Figure of the Year' was not given to an artist, composer, or producer, but to Secretary of State Moerdiono. Attended by high-ranking government ministers and army generals, among other elites, it was 'proof that dangdut had achieved a position of respect: sparkling, well-groomed, and, yes, even prestigious' ('Generasi baru', 1997). Touted as the new generation of dangdut, celebrities walked down the red carpet in evening gowns and suits. The values of the 'new generation' contrasted with the unglamorous, ordinary, and increasingly disordered lives of the majority of its fans.

Dangdut television programs experimented with a variety of formats that revolved around dangdut. Salam Dangdut, a product of MTV Asia that first aired in 1999, featured music videos, interviews with stars, and tips on how to shake one's hips, or *'goyang'* ('Dangdut menggoyang dunia', 1999, p. 5). In addition to music videos, television producers developed dangdut serials (dangdut *sinetron*). 'Balada Dangdut' constructed themes from dangdut songs, an idea that came from Indian films ('Balada dangdut', 1997). Similar to standard sinetron, it featured an attractive star, complicated family situations, a love story, and a rags-to-riches narrative structure.

But what did this 'success' mean as it was reported in popular print media? It meant that the music industry was busy manufacturing dangdut sound recordings, television broadcasts, and popular print media that they imagined would appeal to middle classes and above. Television station RCTI brought in Meggy Z. and Toto Aryo to help attract the 'A-B audience', whose monthly household income was around 1 million rupiah or more per month ('Asyiknya digoyang dangdut', 2001). These stars were hired to help create musical arrangements and themes especially for middle class and elite audiences.

The campaign that 'dangdut was for everyone' was largely a matter of packaging. Dangdut singer and film star Camelia Malik stated:

> I don't want to tell people what to like. I just want to show that dangdut can be wrapped in banana leaves (*daun pisang*) and it can also be wrapped in aluminum foil (*aluminium foil*). It can be put in a box ... Dangdut has been relegated to the lower class. But it turns out that the middle class and above want it too. They said, 'help us out, our tastes need to be satisfied too'. As performers, we have to be able to service anyone and everyone. (Purwanto & Budaya, 2000, p. 6)

If dangdut was for everyone, then why did popular print media concentrate so heavily on representing the wealthy and powerful, the minority of society? As dangdut allegedly began to stand for everyone, the *rakyat* receded even further from representation. This new rhetoric of incorporation contradicted the messages presented in these texts. As a result, the majority of society, who could not identify with the lifestyles represented in these texts, was forced to occupy a position outside these representations.

Dangdut was again the focal point of debates about culture and politics in 2003. Dangdut singer Inul Daratista and her 'drilling dance' (*goyang ngebor*) became immensely popular with dangdut fans even though she had not made a single recording with one of the major commercial recording companies in Indonesia.

It was estimated that several million copies of her VCD (video compact disc) had sold before she was offered a recording contract. The recording and distribution of 'live' Inul concerts enabled television producers in Jakarta to gauge Inul's popularity with dangdut audiences. After seeing spectators' positive reaction to Inul's live performances, producers brought her into the studio to record and broadcast those performances on television stations in Jakarta (Asmarani, 2003).

Inul's trademark dance move was characterized by rapidly moving her hips from side to side, while simultaneously spinning her body up and down. Conservative Islamic groups issued a *fatwa* (edict) against Inul, claiming that her dance moves were pornographic, and therefore forbidden by Islam. These groups issued very New Order-like decrees against Inul, but they were not supported by the central government. The drilling dance found hearty supporters among those groups typically silenced by the Suharto regime: oppositional political groups, the liberal press, intellectuals, and ordinary people.

Due to a more liberal press, politicians, women's rights groups, moderate religious leaders, and intellectuals, along with the voices of conservative Islamic groups, seized on Inul to voice their own ideological positions. In the post-Suharto period, Inulmania contributed to a new dialogic space where conflicting ideological positions could be expressed and debated. The fall of Suharto brought about an expansion of private television stations and popular print media, as well as a loosening of the state's control over media content (Widodo, 2002). As Indonesia moved out from under the shadow of the Suharto era, Inul's body became a stage on which to act out 'rehearsals' for democracy.

In February 2006, women's bodies in general became the target of an anti-pornography bill (RUU-APP, 2006) sponsored by Islamic groups to the Indonesian Legislative Assembly (DPR Indonesia) that would ban people from 'disseminating, listening to, staging, or posting writings, sounds or recorded sounds, film or equivalent, song lyrics, poetry, pictures, photographs and/or paintings that exploit the attraction of the body or body parts of a person dancing or moving in an erotic fashion'. If enacted, this bill will increase the state's authority to regulate women's (and men's) bodies. Dangdut singers, including Inul Daratista as well as many others, represent a challenge to the repressive and authoritarian sponsors of this bill. This legislation will have severe implications for the masses of people captivated by Inul and others, as well as the commercial, government, and critical institutions that represent them.

Conclusion

This brief overview of writing about popular music has shown that 'the people' play a significant role in journalistic writing about Indonesian popular music. In this essay, I have concentrated on the ways in which 'the people' have been constructed within commercial media institutions (music recording, television, popular print media); government institutions (regulatory agencies); and critical institutions (in stories written by critics, academics, and journalists). Of course, actual people read newspapers, listen to music recordings and radio, watch television, and attend concerts. But they have also been produced symbolically as 'the people' through institutions that privilege certain kinds of representations and marginalize others. These institutions have their own hierarchies and internal ideological conflicts, but they all speak on behalf of audiences. In this case, the condition of 'speaking on behalf' is what characterizes asymmetrical relations of power among different groups.

What does it mean to say that dangdut is the music of 'the people'? 'The people' are imagined as embodying certain living spaces, interests, and behaviors. In stories about dangdut, they have been denigrated as backward within elite narratives about economic development and progress. In contrast, liberal intellectuals have used them to mount critiques of modernity. Via dangdut, 'the people' could be harnessed for their sheer numbers in imagining a national culture. And they could be recognized through dangdut as voters during political campaigns. They could also be called into being through commercial television as consumers.

My own participation in the work of representation should not be left unexamined. Throughout this essay, I too have spoken on behalf of 'the people'. I have imagined them as a group excluded from centers of power, a group that requires either protection or intervention from powerful media and government institutions. I have relied on a stereotype of 'the people', those 'who often suffer from injustice inflicted by the rich and powerful' (Heryanto, 1999, p. 162).

The ways in which dangdut has been articulated with the multiple and shifting meanings of 'the people' can help us to understand how mass-mediated popular music has been instrumental in constructing the nature and function of 'the people' in modern Indonesia. Although dangdut's audience was absent as the author of its own representation, its meaning and function took different shapes, and changed over time.

Beyond the invisible fictions about 'the people' constructed in texts inscribed by commercial, government, and critical institutions, however, lies the wild exuberance and pleasure of dangdut. In this space, dangdut does not look forward nor backward, but exists somewhere in the unresolved contradictions of everyday life, signified by mournful lyrics and joyous dancing; hyper-commercialism and strong identification with stars; and entertaining escapist fantasies vs. the banal existence of overcrowded living conditions, oppressively meager working wages, and lack of representation in the public sphere. Beyond the powerful apparatuses that regulate and monitor people's behavior lies an undomesticated space where people can do all sorts of things that would be considered unacceptable according to middle class and elite standards of behavior. In dangdut, this is the space of exaggeration and excess, whether it is the garishness of your outfit, the teasingly erotic way you swing your hips, the vulgar language you use, or the articulation of social issues that cannot be broached in the public sphere. Elites might describe these practices as 'overakting' (from the English 'overacting') because they cross over the boundaries of acceptable behavior. But for dangdut audiences, active participation in a music and dance form that emphasizes openness, spontaneity, and passion represents the heart and soul of what dangdut is all about.

Acknowledgements

For comments on earlier drafts I am grateful to Richard Fox, Andreas Harsono, Mark Hobart, Philip Kitley, Jennifer Lindsay, Goenawan Mohamad, R. Anderson Sutton, and Philip Yampolsky. Due to space limitations, I was not able to include the original Indonesian-language quotes, but I would be happy to send them to anyone who is interested (anwein@pitt.edu).

Notes

[1] A 'kampung' is a neighborhood that can be located in either a village, town, or city. However, '*kampungan*' does not simply describe a person's living space, but it connotes inferiority, backwardness, nonrefinement, lack of formal education, and a low position in a hierarchical ordering of social classes.

[2] This essay is part of a larger research project I am conducting on the social and musical history of dangdut in Indonesia. The number of English-language scholarly articles, theses and dissertations, and working papers about the genre is surprisingly low, scattered across the disciplines of history (Frederick, 1982), music (Hatch, 1985; Yampolsky, 1991), anthropology (Simatupang, 1996; Wallach, 2002) and Asian studies (Pioquinto, 1995 and 1998; Sen and Hill, 2000; Browne, 2000).

[3] Both polls excluded Global TV, which broadcasts numerous music programs (including MTV Asia) that are not specific to genre, as well as the dangdut program *Salam Dangdut*. I conducted the first informal poll based on the weekly schedule, 5–11 June 2006. The second poll was reported in Agus Irkham (2005).

[4] My findings are based on a review of over 400 articles about dangdut, representing 45 different publications, written between 1972 and 2006.

[5] During the revolutionary period (1945–1949), the *rakyat* referred to the followers of a leader, in this case, Sukarno, who was the voice of the people (literally an 'extension of the tongue of the people', 'penyambung lidah *rakyat* Indonesia') (Anderson, 1990, p. 62). According to James Siegel, the *rakyat* ceased to exist in the New Order because Suharto did not speak for or to them (Siegel, 1998, p. 4). Nevertheless, popular understandings of the *rakyat* still exist as 'the innocent, morally superior, economically unprivileged but politically sovereign figures who often suffer from injustice inflicted by the rich and powerful' (Heryanto, 1999, p. 162).

[6] Sociologists prefer the plural form 'middle classes' in order to reflect the different and contradictory elements that constitute members of this socioeconomic grouping (see Dick, 1985; Gerke, 2000; Heryanto, 1999, 2003; Lev, 1990; Robison, 1996).

[7] In a classic formulation, Raymond Williams (1961) writes that there are no masses, only ways of seeing people as masses (p. 289).

[8] Its 'nasal, ornamented vocal style, the proletarian character of its mass audience, and its association with sinful and otherwise disreputable activities' suggest comparisons with Algerian rai and Turkish Arabesque (Wallach, 2002). Other elements of these comparisons include hybrid musical style, Islamic associations, and primarily male fan base in live concert settings.

[9] Gender in dangdut has been discussed in Pioquinto (1995); Browne (2000); and Wallach (2002).

[10] The origin of the term 'dangdut' is discussed further in the following section.

[11] See Pioquinto (1998) for a good discussion of the rock-*irama melayu* conflict and the cultural politics of labeling genres (pp. 79–84).

[12] Managing editor Remy Sylado claimed that the word 'dangdut' first appeared in print in *Aktuil* in 1972 (Pioquinto, 1998, p. 77). But, after reviewing all of the issues for that year, I was not able to find the citation. The first written reference that I have found is in 'Dunia Ellya Khadam' (1972, p. 36). It was around this time that rock musician Benny Subardja, a member of the band Giant Step, characterized dangdut as *'musik tai anjing'* ('dog shit music'; Frederick, 1982, pp. 60, 124).

[13] An example of *cengeng* lyrics in a dangdut song is 'Bunuh aku dengan cintamu' ('Kill me with your love'). 'Porno' lyrics can be seen in songs including 'Salome', 'Judul-Judulan', and 'Minta Ajimat'. Lyrics for the latter are: 'I'm bored/singing in the bathroom/grinning/grimacing alone, laughing alone, ejaculating alone' (*'Bosan-bosan begini/Nyanyi di kamar mandi/Meringis sendiri, tertawa sendiri, keluar sendiri'*).

[14] Dangdut had played a role in elections since at least 1977, when artists were involved in government campaigning. I would like to thank Philip Kitley for alerting me to a newspaper photo with the caption 'Artists from the kampung' showing media personalities H. Oma Irama (Rhoma Irama), Harry Roesli, Benyamin, Iskak, Kris Biantoro, and Ateng (*Kompas*, 1977, 7 April, p. 1). Both Golkar and the PPP used dangdut to mobilize the populace in various election campaigns in 1982 (Frederick, 1982).

References

Anderson, B. (1990). *Language and power: Exploring political cultures in Indonesia*. Ithaca: Cornell University Press.

Aribowo, B. (1983, December 8). Proklamasi identitas. *Fokus*, 16–17.

Aribowo, B. (2002). Tiada pesta tanpa dangdut. *Pantau*, 25. Retrieved June 20, 2005, from www.pantau.or.id/txt/26/17c.html

Asmarani, D. (2003, March 9). A village girl shakes it up. *Straits Times* (Singapore).

Asyiknya digoyang dangdut. (2001, September 9). *Kompas*.

Balada dangdut, berpangkal dari lagu. (1997, September 10). *Kompas*.

Barraud, A. (2003, April 22). Indonesia: Pornography or performance? *ABC News Radio (Asia Pacific)*. Retrieved August 9, 2004, from http://www.abc.net.au/ra/asiapac/programs/s836743.htm

Basofi Sudirman: Dengan dangdut kita sukseskan pembangunan. (1994, May 30–June 5). *Citra, 218*, 2.

Berjuang dalam goyang. (1989). *Matra*, 13–22.

Browne, S. (2000). *The gender implications of dangdut kampungan: Indonesian 'low-class' popular music*. Centre of Southeast Asian Studies, Monash University Working Paper No. 109. Monash, Australia: Monash Asia Institute.

Dangdut goyang terus pop kok loyo. (1992, May 16). *Tempo*, 108.

Dangdut menggoyang dunia. (1999, January 31). *Pos Kota*, 5.

Dangdut siang bolong TPI kupas tuntas persoalan. (1995). *Pos Film*.

Dangdut, setelah halal di TV-RI. (1979, May 5). *Tempo*, 50–54.

Dick, H. W. (1985). The rise of a middle class and the changing concept of equity in Indonesia: An interpretation. *Indonesia, 39*, 71–92.

Dua orang raja. (1978, January 14). *Tempo*, 41–43.

Dunia Ellya Khadam. (1972, May 27). *Tempo*, 36.

Emha, A. N. (1979, June 7). Jiwa dangdut kita pada dasarnya sangat besar. *Aktuil*, 16.

Frederick, W. (1982). Rhoma Irama and the dangdut style: Aspects of contemporary Indonesian popular culture. *Indonesia, 34*, 102–130.

Generasi baru, dangdut dut ... (1997, July 16–22). *Tabloid Berita Mingguan Adil*, 40.

Gerke, S. (2000). Global lifestyles under local conditions: The new Indonesian middle class. In C. Beng-huat (Ed.), *Consumption in Asia: Lifestyles and Identities* (pp. 135–158). London: Routledge.

Giliran musik dangdut dikecam. (1992, November 8). *Suara Pembaruan*.

Goyang dangdut. (1991, May 25). *Tempo*, 49–66.

Hak Asasi Dilarang. (1977, December 17). *Tempo*, 17–18.

Harahap, R. (1994). Pesta demokrasi praktisi dangdut mencari figure pemimpin. *Jayakarta, 2124*, 5.

Hatch, M. (1985). Popular music in Indonesia. In S. Frith (Ed.), *World music, politics and social change* (pp. 47–67). Manchester: Manchester University Press.

Heryanto, A. (1999). The years of living luxuriously: Identity politics of Indonesia's new rich. In M. Pinches (Ed.), *Culture and privilege in capitalist Asia* (pp. 159–187). London: Routledge.

Heryanto, A. (2003). Public intellectuals, media and democratization: Cultural politics of the middle classes in Indonesia. In A. Heryanto, & S. Mandal (Eds.), *Challenging authoritarianism in Southeast Asia* (pp. 24–59). New York: RoutledgeCurzon.

Irkham, A. M. (2005, July 18). Televisi, kaya laba miskin wacana. *Suara Merdeka*. Retrieved June 12, 2006, from www.suaramerdeka.com/harian/0507/18/opi4.html

Kitley, P. (2000). *Television, nation, and culture in Indonesia.* Athens: Ohio University Press.

Lagi ngetrend, lagu asing 'diterjemahkan'. (July 7, 1991). *Nova, 176*, 10.

Lev, D. (1990). Notes on the middle class and change in Indonesia. In R. Tanter & K. Young (Eds.), *The politics of middle class Indonesia*. Monash Papers on Southeast Asia No. 19 (pp. 44–48). Clayton, Victoria: Centre of Southeast Asian Studies, Monash University.

Lindsay, J. (1995). Cultural policy and the performing arts in Southeast Asia. *Bijdragen: Tot de taal-, land-, en volkenkunde, 151*, 656–671.

Miloer, M. (1978, July 31). Serangkaian show Pretty Sisters & Surya Group di Malang. SAS Group di Semarang. *Aktuil, 251*, 52–53.

Moerdiono dan Habibie berjoget ria. (1992, May 24). *Pos Kota*.

Pedoman dangdut berasal dari Melayu. (1994, November 20). *Pos Film, 126*, 4.

Penayangan dangdut di TVRI diperketat. (1992, February 4). *Kompas*.

Pioquinto, C. (1995). Dangdut at sekaten: Female representations in live performance. *Review of Indonesian and Malaysian Affairs, 29*, 59–90.

Pioquinto, C. (1998). A musical hierarchy reordered: Dangdut and the rise of a popular music. *Asian Cultural Studies, 24*, 73–125.

Piper, S. (1995). Performances for fifty years of Indonesian independence: Articles from the Indonesian press (T. Day & S. Piper, Trans). *Review of Indonesian and Malaysian Affairs, 1 & 2*, 37–58.

Purwanto, G. S., & Budaya, P. (2000, July). Camelia Malik: 'Sudah saatnya dangdut Go International'. *Pro-TV, 2*, 6.

Rhoma Irama ... Sampai titik darah yang penghabisan. (1987, October 20). *Mutiara, 7*, 19–25.

Robison, R. (1996). The middle class and the bourgeoisie in Indonesia. In R. Robison, & D. Goodman (Eds.), *The new rich in Asia* (pp. 79–104). London: Routledge.

RUU-APP (Anti-pornography bill, 2006). A. K. Cohen & M. I. Cohen (Trans.).

Satria berdakwah, raja dari bawah. (1984, June 30). *Tempo*, 27–33.

Sen, K., & Hill, D. (2000). *Media, culture and politics in Indonesia*. South Melbourne: Oxford University Press.

Siegel, J. (1998). *A new criminal type in Jakarta: Counter-revolution today*. Durham, NC: Duke University Press.

Simatupang, G. R. L. L. (1996). *The development of dangdut and its meanings: A study of popular music in Indonesia*. Master's thesis, Department of Anthropology and Sociology, Monash University, Victoria.

Soemardi, I. (1979, June 7). Estimasi pasaran kaset di Indonesia. *Aktuil, 16*, 40.

Steele, J. (2005). *Wars within: The story of Tempo, an independent magazine in Soeharto's Indonesia.* Jakarta: Equinox Publishing.

Sutton, R. A. (2003). Local, global, or national? Popular music on Indonesian television. In S. Kumar, & L. Parks (Eds.), *Planet TV: A world television reader* (pp. 320–340). New York: New York University Press.

Suyitno, A. (1991, January 20). Musik dangdut dan kelebihannya. *Pos film, 928*, 33.

Wallach, J. (2002). *Modern noise and ethnic accents: Indonesian popular music in the era of Reformasi.* Doctoral dissertation, University of Pennsylvania, Philadelphia.

Widodo, A. (2002). Consuming passions. *Inside Indonesia.* Retrieved May 30, 2006, from www.insideindonesia.org/edit72/Theme%20-%20Amrih.html

Williams, R. (1961). *Culture and society.* Harmondsworth: Penguin.

Williams, S. (1989). Current developments in Sundanese popular music. *Asian Music, 21*, 105–136.

Yampolsky, P. (1989). Hati yang luka: An Indonesian hit. *Indonesia, 47*, 1–17.

Yampolsky, P. (1991). Indonesian popular music: Kroncong, dangdut, and langgam Jawa. *Music of Indonesia Series, 2*, Liner Notes to Smithsonian/Folkways SF 40056.

Yampolsky, P. (1995). Forces for change in the regional performing arts of Indonesia. *Bijdragen: Tot de taal-, land-, en volkenkunde, 151*, 700–725.

Yurnaldi & Rakaryan, S. (1997, July 13). Musik dangdut mencapai puncaknya. *Kompas*, 20.

Zurbuchen, M. (1990). Images of culture and development in Indonesia: The Cockroach Opera. *Asian Theatre Journal, 7*, 127–149.

Afterword

Richard Fox

So, what is this thing called entertainment? How is it related to mass media? And why might this relationship be relevant to scholarship on contemporary Indonesia? Each of the four articles contained in this special issue implies a partial answer to these questions. In this brief afterword, I wish to pull at a few of the critical threads that both hold these articles together and suggest the possibility of their unraveling. Far from undercutting the importance of the arguments presented by our authors, I propose that this potential for unraveling—or, to switch metaphors, for unsettling the philosophical foundations on which they are based—implies both their originality as well as the radicality of their implications for future research on mass media in general, and on Indonesian entertainment media in particular.

As Mark Hobart notes in the 'Introduction' to this special issue, our point of departure has already landed us in critical trouble, as there is no self-evident reason to start from the assumption that 'entertainment' makes for a viable cross-cultural category. If we can assume, for instance, that entertainment is in a significant sense constituted by what it is *not*, following one of the fundamental insights of structuralist analysis, we might then be forced to consider more closely its opposition to any number of categories, including perhaps most importantly that of 'work' or 'labor'. Given that the social uses and significance of labor have themselves been anything but constant through the ages and across the globe (Marx and Engels, *passim*), arguably the same could be said of categories like 'entertainment' that are constituted in opposition to it. Asad has argued an analogous case for both 'religion' (1993) and 'the secular' (2003), demonstrating that the social significance of, and mutual relations between, these two categories have undergone a series of transformations through different historical periods. And it is hard to imagine why entertainment should be any different. Given the great historical variation in economic, social and political relations across—let alone beyond—Southeast Asia (e.g. Day, 2002), it should be the regularities, rather than the disjunctures, between Southeast Asian and Euro-American forms of life that require explanation.

Idol Thoughts

With this in mind, let me begin with one such regularity. It turns out that 'talent quest' programs look unmistakably similar whether one is watching in Indonesia (*Indonesian Idol*), Britain (*Pop Idol*) or America (*American Idol*). And, as Coutas explains ('Fame, fortune, *fantasi*'), this is no simple accident of fad or fashion. Rather, it is the deliberate—and rigorously managed—result of transnationally franchised television production. She argues, '[i]n many ways, the format itself, and not the people working within it, constitutes the most powerful cultural inter-mediary' (Coutas, this issue, p. 371). So, with the resounding success of the 'Idol' format in such culturally disparate countries,[1] it would appear that we are seeing the emergence of a very particular—and, importantly, transnational—configuration of capital, mass media and popular culture.

Such observations have conventionally been the cue for one or another variation on the theme of 'globalization', with its attendant—and broadly liberal—concerns regarding the consequences of Western power abroad. Although the problem has often been represented in terms of the deleterious 'effects' on local peoples, cultures and economies, in more recent years denizens of 'the local' (read: economically less-powerful places and nations) have increasingly been attributed by scholars with some form of agency in their encounters with 'the global'. In the latter accounts, people of 'developing' nations are generally offered some degree of recognition as being actively engaged in the kinds of 'meaning-making' and 'identity-formation' previously thought to be the preserve of those privileged enough to live in the 'developed' world.

Underpinning this debate is a permutation of the (suspiciously Manichean) opposition of structure vs. agency that has long dogged the human sciences. In other words: does a given instantiation of 'global culture' determine the form and consequences of its local manifestations? (= Structure, and so Bad.) Or do regional appropriations of 'global culture' transform it into something new and authentically local? (= Agency, and so Good.) In our case, the critical dilemma might be rephrased more specifically as follows: are Indonesians—as political subjects—*determining* the terms in which they engage with the 'Idol' phenomenon, or are they *determined* by it?

Coutas concludes that one's evaluation depends on what is emphasized: the popularity of the program—and the format more generally—may seem to provide evidence of cultural and economic imperialism; yet, at the same time, the program might also be described as a case of 'feeling glocal' (see Iwabuchi, 2004), the active expression of (local) Indonesian particularity in the idiom of a (globally) universal format. But can *Indonesian Idol* really be both at once? And, if so, how are these two evaluations analytically related to one another?

On the Importance of Being Élite

Let us consider the conditions under which our dilemma has arisen. Why might agency (or its absence) be of such critical importance to scholarship on Indonesian media? Both Hobart ('Entertaining illusions') and Weintraub ('Dangdut soul') provide insightful analyses of the various ways in which different kinds of audiences have been discursively relieved of the ability to understand and comment on their own lives. Both authors stress that such representations of 'the audience' cannot be mapped onto actual viewers and listeners. But implicit in their analyses is the idea that these are *misrepresentations* that are also not without consequence. Perhaps for this reason, in his concluding remarks, Weintraub ('Dangdut soul') draws our attention to the context in which he is writing ('I too have spoken on behalf of "the people". I have imagined them as a group excluded from centers of power'; Weintraub, this issue, p. 411). This is an important point. But I think it can be pushed further, to recognize that such scholarly expressions of concern are themselves a key component of an élite discourse comparable to that explored both by him and by Hobart in their respective contributions to this volume.

Op-eds and editorials in Indonesian newspapers and magazines may frequently express an earnest concern for the fate of the benighted masses, with their insatiable appetite for all things violent, erotic, supernatural and otherwise opposed to reason and the progress of the nation. But, as Weintraub rightly notes, these decidedly paternalistic accounts are of little relevance to the lives of the people they purport to represent. After all, as we have seen in the case of dangdut, they are published in newspapers and magazines 'that most dangdut fans would never read, sandwiched between advertisements for products that most dangdut fans would never consume' (Weintraub, this issue, p. 411).

The scholarly analogy here is almost too obvious to mention. For instance, how many of those deemed 'subaltern' are actually aware of, let alone have any use for, what is said in *Subaltern studies*? Hobart makes a related point about a prominent Indonesian commentator's concern that popular TV programs about the 'supernatural' may cause the nation's children to 'think that life can improve without learning or even working hard' (Hobart, this issue, p. 393). However, as Hobart points out, the élite's concern in this connection would be more appropriately directed toward their own children than to the overwhelming majority of Indonesians that make up the country's dispersed and heterogeneous underclasses for whom, 'however hard they study or work, the supernatural arguably offers at least as rational and realistic a chance of success' (Hobart, this issue, p. 393).

The question I wish to raise in this connection is whether we are justified in extrapolating from Hobart's observation to make a similar argument regarding scholars' own expressed concerns for the underprivileged and misrepresented. With academic labor feeling the pinch under the growing pressure of a management culture focused on the bottom line, scholars' concerns for 'the masses' are beginning to look suspiciously similar to concerns they may have for their own well-being. In brief: an increasingly competitive academic job market—and what that entails for those lucky enough to find stable employment—leaves many faculty members (as an intellectual proletariat?) feeling that their lives are determined in significant ways by political and economic processes beyond their comprehension, let alone control.

Given the circumstances, finding current scholarship on mass media to be so thoroughly skewered on the forked dilemma of 'structure' vs. 'agency' makes for a rather ironic twist on an old debate to which I shall return in a moment.[2]

My primary point in raising the question of the scholarly context is not so much that professional circumstances exhaustively explain an otherwise laudable concern for 'the masses'. The genealogy for this orientation is decidedly more complex, and warrants careful and sustained consideration in its own right. Here I simply wish to point out that the now near-obligatory statement of concern for properly representing the 'agency' of the inadequately privileged often has about as much to do with their lives as an Indonesian politician's opinion on dangdut has to do with the day-to-day lives of those who actually listen to the music in *kampungs* from Sabang to Merauke. And this should be of no little importance to a set of disciplines that have traditionally aspired to social (and often political) relevance.

Practice: A Critical Difference

Returning briefly to *Indonesian Idol*, I should emphasize that I agree in general terms with Coutas' concluding assessment: specifically, that what we are seeing with the transnational dissemination of the 'Idol' format is neither 'global' nor 'local', but rather 'something else again' (Coutas, this issue, p. 371). However, it is not altogether clear what that alternative 'something' might look like. On closer inspection, there appears to be a degree of critical slippage occurring in the movement between her two evaluations—specifically pertaining to the nature of the object of study—and I believe a comparison with Barkin's analysis ('The foreignizing gaze') may help to clarify some of the issues.

If Coutas distinguishes between two possible evaluations of *Indonesian Idol*, Barkin is also faced with an important disjuncture—albeit one of a somewhat different kind. In his analysis of the Indonesian program *Anak Muda Punya Mau*, he notes that there are important differences between, on the one hand, the Indonesian program as envisaged by its producers and, on the other, the Euro-American formats on which they drew in creating it.

Although the Indonesian producers of *Anak Muda* drew heavily on 'certain aesthetic and narrative aspects of foreign [travel] programs', they 'did not concern themselves with the internal logic of [these] shows' (Barkin, this issue, p. 352). In other words, their use of these British and American programs probably had little to do with what the original producers in the UK and US had envisaged. Here we may note the structural analogy between this disjuncture and that with their own ideal audience. For, as Barkin points out, there is no easy fit between the vast majority of *Anak Muda*'s likely viewers and the 'foreignizing gaze' that is characteristic of 'the audience' as it is positioned by the program itself.

This lack of equivalence between the viewers of a program and its ideal addressee is, of course, hardly unique to Indonesia. But it does raise the important question of how producers, programs and viewers are related to one another critically.

Conventionally speaking, these are generally recognized as three of the key components of a 'communicative' process. However, it is at precisely this point— i.e. the point of critically linking the moments of 'production' and 'reception' in a unified process—that we see the slippage that I mentioned at the beginning of this section. What is the nature of this slippage? And why is it such a problem?

As Hobart suggests in his editorial 'Introduction', the model of mass mediation that is generally presupposed—in cultural and media studies, as well as in mass communications—leaves something to be desired. Simply put, their analyses ride on a weak theory of practice, in which entities such as text, meaning or 'the message' are assumed to exist both absolutely and prior to those occasions on which they are interpreted, 'decoded' or otherwise used. This approach requires that one assume *a priori* that the respective worlds of production and viewing are both determinate and commensurate. In other words: the analyst must take it as given that the actions of producers and viewers—though superficially different—are coherently rooted at a more fundamental level in a unifying set of mutually-consistent presuppositions regarding the nature of meaning, reason and intelligibility, the purposes of viewing, etc. On such an account, interpretations might differ from one viewer to the next (and also, as we have seen, between producers and viewers), but the *possibilities* for interpretation—and other uses—would ultimately be limited by the (propositional) 'content' of their object, usually imagined as a 'media text'.

This critical commitment to something akin to the 'media text' is what holds 'media studies' together as a discipline. (Without the coherence of its object, it would merely be 'Studies'.) However, it is also a classic example of philosophical substantialism (Collingwood, 1946). That is, it rides on the assumption that there exists a pre-discursive essence—or 'substance'—that unifies the various moments in its own historical transformation. (The latter would include, for example, the interpretations or 'decodings' of particular viewers.) However, unlike their hermeneutic counterparts in older (and often literary) disciplines, media scholars seem to have paid scant attention to the inherent circularity of the interpretive process as it is configured on the basis of this model. The interpretation of a text rides on prior knowledge of its context, while prior knowledge of context requires the interpretation of the very texts through which it is known. And so, in order to begin the dialectical movement between text and context, one must begin with what amounts to an interpretive leap of faith. This is, in part, a trace of the legacy bequeathed to hermeneutics—and, eventually, on to media scholarship—by theology and biblical studies (Fox, 2000).

Despite the inherent philosophical problems (Fox, 2003), one presumes this approach is 'methodologically' appealing not only for its happy agreement with 'common sense', but also for its foreclosure on the awkward consequences that arise from acknowledging irreducible difference (see below). Yet, as the contributions to this volume suggest, the facts—both philosophically and empirically—are stacked against it. Whether cast in terms of 'producers' and 'consumers' or, alternatively, 'senders' and 'receivers' (see Hobart's 'Introduction'), the model rides on a constitutive—and ultimately theologically-derived—metaphor of a subtle substance moving through space. Quite literally 'transmission' is a 'sending across'. In addition to inherent problems of internal consistency, serious empirical research—like that presented in this volume—merely further highlights both the degree and frequency of the disjunctures that emerge between what are conventionally—if misleadingly—understood in terms of 'production' and 'reception'.[3]

Get Real

Scholarly faith in substance underwrites the possibility of interpretation—and, perhaps more importantly, the possibility of *understanding*—by limiting difference to degree, as opposed to kind.[4] The question is how we are to go about accounting for those actions that, on the face of it, seem anything but amenable to analysis in terms commensurate with academic discourse. Weintraub, for instance, notes that although 'the audience' for dangdut has long been fodder for commentary from the élite, the world of its actual listeners is something quite apart. He suggests, the 'heart and soul of what dangdut is all about' is the 'openness, spontaneity, and passion' that constitutes a certain 'undomesticated space' that is beyond the reach of the elite (Weintraub, this issue, p. 411). Hobart makes a similar point with respect to the worlds depicted in *kriminal* and *mistik* programming. But how is scholarship—arguably the very epitome of domestication—to position itself in relation to these forms of social life?

On reflection it seems that to acknowledge a radical disjuncture that is simultaneously irreducible would logically entail forfeiting our default position of epistemological privilege. And we then would be left in the rather awkward predicament of discerning the value of an 'expert' knowledge that is incapable of comprehending its object (at least in any traditional sense of the word). These are serious issues and, if properly understood, have far-reaching implications for even the most empirically-minded research. For, in fact, what is at issue is the very nature of 'the empirical' itself.

As one solution to this predicament, Hobart proposes what amounts to a Levinasian inflection of Bakhtinian dialogue. And I think this is one of the more attractive options on offer. On this approach, as I understand it, one would try in one's work to recognize the Other not merely as an object but, rather, as a subject capable of knowing and commenting on her own history and position in the world, as well as on the conditions of inquiry and the subject of the inquirer. Among other things, this would open up the possibility for cross-cultural questioning, if not necessarily a guarantee of understanding. Of course it also opens up the possibility of refusal. Ice Cube, the well-known American rap star, is reported to have refused to include lyrics in the liner notes of his records. The reason: he said he did not want them to be subjected to analysis by the white bourgeois intelligentsia. So, a more dialogic model may have its advantages, but it also comes with its own set of problems. Given the multiple disjunctures that constitute 'mass media', not least among these is the possibility that we end up with an ethnographic analogue to reality TV which, as Hobart notes, is characterized by 'scrupulously avoiding reality, while claiming the opposite' (Hobart, this issue, p. 343).

Acknowledgements

My thanks go to both Mark Hobart and Judith Fox for their comments on an earlier draft of these remarks.

Notes

[1] See *Wikipedia* (http://en.wikipedia.org/wiki/Idol_series; accessed 23 July 2006) for details on the 'Idol' programs that are currently on the air internationally.
[2] The problem dates back at least to the 19th century, with the various economic (e.g. Marx), sociological (e.g. Durkheim) and psychological (e.g. Freud) attempts to grapple with the legacy of Kant.
[3] It is worth noting that the *terminology* associated with this model (e.g. 'reception') is hegemonic to the point that it becomes difficult to avoid replicating it in critiques. That is to say, for the sake of intelligibility, one is often forced to adopt the very language that one wishes to subvert.
[4] In other words, on this basis, difference is always already reduced to a foundational—and knowable—sameness. One might compare, for instance, the New Order articulation of religious difference in which that 'difference' is ultimately subordinate to the deeper unity implied by a notionally universal adherence to one of the five state-sanctioned forms of monotheistic belief. On this account, 'difference' says more about similarity than it does about difference.

References

Asad, T. (1993). *Genealogies of religion: Disciplines and reasons of power in Christianity and Islam*. Baltimore & London: Johns Hopkins University Press.
Asad, T. (2003). *Formations of the secular: Christianity, Islam, modernity*. Stanford: Stanford University Press.
Collingwood, R. G. (1946). *The idea of history*. Oxford: Oxford University Press.
Day, A. (2002). *Fluid iron: State formation in Southeast Asia*. Honolulu: University of Hawaii Press.
Fox, R. (2000). Forget the appearances! Some thoughts from a Copernican in TV land. Retrieved July 20, 2006, from www.berubah.org/forgettheappearances.pdf
Fox, R. (2003). Substantial transmissions: A presuppositional analysis of 'the Old Javanese text' as an object of knowledge, and its implications for the study of religion in Bali. *Bijdragen tot de Taal-,Land- en Volkenkunde, 159*(1), 65–107.
Iwabuchi, K. (2004). Feeling glocal: Japan in the global television format business. In A. Moran, & M. Keane (Eds.), *Television across Asia: Television industries, programme formats and globalization* (pp. 21–35). London: RoutledgeCurzon.

Index

active viewing 33
advertising 25
aesthetic reductionism 12
Aktuil 60, 65
Anak Muda Punya Mau 3
Anderson, B. 66
Appadurai, A. 31
audiences 55–7
authenticity; and exoticism 12

Bakhtin, M. M. 57
Baudrillard, J. 57
BBC (British Broadcasting Corporation) 11,
   14–15
Becker, A. 57
Bernstein, B. xi
Bourdieu, P. 30

celebrity 21–39
'celetoids' 22
censorship 44; New Order and
   Dangdut 66–7
clawback; hierarchy of 46
consumerism 61
cosmopolitan globalism 16
crime programmes 45–7
cultural bumpering 14
cultural capital 30
cultural homogenization 17
cultural hybridity 38
cultural imperialism 28–30
cultural pluralism 38
cultural self-representation 6
culturalist approaches to Indonesian
   media ix

Dangdut 60–77; and New Order censorship
   66–7; relationship with Indonesian rock
   65; stylistic definition 63–4
Daratista, I. 75

Deery, J. 26
'dumbing down' 29

economic component of media
   imperialism 30
emancipation 56
entertainment; definition of 81
escapism xii
exoticism; and authenticity 12

fatwa 75
foreignizing gaze xiii, 1–17
Frederick, W. 67–8
FremantleMedia 23

Gabriel, T. 6
Gazali, E. 54
globalization 31, 82
globalism; cosmopolitan 16

Hall, S. xi, 33
hybridity; cultural 38

Idola 21–39; sign system 27–8
imperialism; cultural and media 28–30
imported television formats 24
Indonesian Broadcasting Commission
   (KPI) 44
Indonesian culture; celebrification of 22
Indonesian Idol 21–39, 82
Indonesian rock; relationship with
   Dangdut 65
Indonesian Sound Recording Industry
   Association 61
interactivity 36–8
Irama, R. 63, 67
Ishadi 54
Islam 75
Islamic Opposition Party (PPP) 67
Iwabuchi, K. 31

Jakarta xiii, 63, 75

Kitley, P. 33
Kompas 52
Kriminal 42–57

labour xii
leisure xii
lifestyle: modelling 11; programming 2
light entertainment programming 4;
    morality of 8
local food; representation in travel
    programs 12

magazine: *Aktuil* 60, 65; *Mutiara* 68; *Tempo*
    64, 67, 69, 71–2
Malik, C. 74
masses 55
masyarakat 52–3, 55
media; culturalist approaches to ix
media imperialism 28–30; economic
    component of 30
Mistik 42–57
modernity 6, 50, 54, 76
Moerdiono 71–2, 73
Mohamad, G. 72
Moran, A. 32
Mulvey, L. 14–15
music; Indonesian popular 60–77
Mutiara 68

National Geographic 15
nationalism 66; Indonesian 66
New Order; end of 44
New Order censorship; and Dangdut 66–7
New Order regime propaganda viii
newspaper: *Kompas* 52; *Pos Kota* 71;
    Republika 52

occult programmes 45

Palapa viii
Percaya Nggak Percaya 51
pluralism; cultural 38
political talk shows x
Pop Idol 21
popular music 60–77; Indonesian 60–77;
    reinvigoration of 32

Pos Kota 71
postcolonialism 6
poverty 4
product placement 26
programming; lifestyle 2
propaganda: of New Order regime viii;
    of Suharto regime 44
Puspa, T. 65

rakyat 55
RCTI 23
reality television 21–39, 42–57; supernatural
    48–50, *see also* television
Republika 52
Rojek, C. 22

Saudi Arabia 55
Schiller, H. 28
self-representation; cultural 6
Sen, K. 6
sinetron 13
sinetron Wah Cantiknya! 16
Singapore; Orchard Road 10
souvenirs 11
Sreberny-Mohammadi, A. 31
Sudirman, B. 71
Suharto, President viii
Suharto regime; propaganda 44
supernatural reality shows 48–50
surveillance 44

telephone call voting 34
television: industry deregulation 70;
    viewing x, *see also* light entertainment
    programming; reality television; travel
    programs
Tempo 64, 67, 69, 71–2
Thompson, J. 30
traditional; symbols of the 1–17
transnationalism 6
TransTV 1–17, 54
travel programs 3; backpacker oriented 8;
    types of 7–13

violence 50

Western travel programs; types of 7–13
Widodo, A. 22

For Product Safety Concerns and Information please contact our EU representative GPSR@taylorandfrancis.com Taylor & Francis Verlag GmbH, Kaufingerstraße 24, 80331 München, Germany

Batch number: 08153807

Printed by Printforce, the Netherlands